CAPITAL LIVES

PROFILES OF 32 LEADING OTTAWA PERSONALITIES

By Valerie Knowles

Book Coach Press

Ottawa, 2005

Capital Lives

Profiles of 32 Leading Ottawa Personalities

© 2005, Valerie Knowles

Valerie Knowles
knowles@istar.ca

Published by Book Coach Press
www.BookCoachPress.com

Care has been taken to trace the ownership of copyright material used in this book. The author and the publisher welcome any information enabling them to rectify any references or credit in subsequent editions.

Printed and bound in Canada.

Editors: Serena Williamson, Sigrid Macdonald
Design: D. Lanouette
Printer: Tri-Co Group

Library and Archives Canada Cataloguing in Publication

Knowles, Valerie
    Capital lives : 32 profiles of leading Ottawa personalities / Valerie Knowles.

Includes bibliographical references and index.
ISBN 0-9739071-1-8

1. Ottawa (Ont.)--Biography. 2. Canada--Biography. I. Title.

FC3096.25.K56 2005   971.3'84'0099   C2005-905529-4

CAPITAL
LIVES

TABLE OF CONTENTS

MAYORS

MPS AND JUDGES

PHILANTHROPISTS

PHYSICIANS

PUBLIC SERVANTS

PREFACE

All the profiles in this collection have been published previously in the Ottawa edition of *Forever Young*, a seniors' publication. Some of the pieces have been modified since publication, but only in minor respects and then usually in the interests of accuracy and clarity.

On glancing at the table of contents, some readers will wonder why certain choices were made. In reply, all I can say is that a particular person interested me, was dead, and had made a substantial contribution to the Ottawa community. In order to write a 1,000-word piece on this figure, however, I had to have access to sufficient documentation. If it wasn't available, this alone was often enough to reject a certain subject for profiling.

Valerie Knowles

ACKNOWLEDGEMENTS

As with every book, large or small, this one required the help of numerous people. To Jayne Anderson, the editor of *Forever Young's* Ottawa edition, I owe a vote of thanks for responding positively to my suggestion for a series of articles on well-known Ottawans from the past. I would also like to thank Serena Williamson, president of Book Coach Press, for warmly embracing the idea of this book and for overseeing every stage of the publication process.

I am grateful to Dr. John Taylor for his helpful suggestions regarding the introductions to each section, to Sigrid Macdonald for her editing expertise, and to the late Cyntia Durance for reading the manuscript and making useful comments. I would like to thank Donald Lanouette for the excellent job he did on the graphics and Barbara McInnes, Grete Hale and David Bullock for kindly providing me with testimonials. Last, but not least, I owe a debt of gratitude to my husband, David, who, as usual in such undertakings, furnished the necessary computer expertise and to Clive Pyne for compiling a comprehensive index.

Valerie Knowles, Ottawa, September 2005

INTRODUCTION

Ottawans owe Valerie Knowles a debt of gratitude for searching and recording on paper for our enlightenment, the lives of 32 well-known citizens from the past. What riches she has uncovered about these remarkable men and women, and what they did to build the cornerstones and fabric of our community.

This informative book will leave a legacy for Ottawa of what these citizens have done to enrich and preserve, not only our city, but also the whole of humanity.

Grete Hale, BJ, GCLJ, FHSC, FRCGS, CMLJ

Chairman Emeritus Morrison Lamothe Inc.

CREATIVE ARTISTS

Not until after Ottawa had progressed from a young, pioneering society to a more mature one did culture begin to figure at all in the city's English and French communities. Even then it led a very tenuous existence. Moreover until the First World War, the capital's intellectual reputation owed much to civil servants who came to Ottawa to work for the federal government (an outstanding example is the poet Duncan Campbell Scott, profiled in this section) and to British governors-generals and their wives, who lent their patronage to music, drama, a National Gallery and a Royal Society.

Only in recent decades has Ottawa developed a lively arts scene, aided and abetted by such artists as Victor Tolgesy, the well-known sculptor, and writers, whose ranks have included Irene Spry, the economist and historian. Both are profiled in this section.

DUNCAN CAMPBELL SCOTT
CELEBRATED POET AND GOVERNMENT ADMINISTRATOR

(1862-1947)

—————■—————

When Duncan Campbell Scott died in Ottawa on December 19, 1947, the *Evening Citizen* hailed him as the "uncrowned poet Laureate of Canada."

This shy, tall, angular man was not just a distinguished Canadian poet, however. He was also a short-story writer, one of the prime movers in the establishment of the Dominion Drama Festival and the Ottawa Little Theatre, and a government mandarin who helped to enforce a harsh assimilation policy against Canada's native people.

The son of William Scott, an itinerant Methodist minister, Duncan Campbell Scott was born in Ottawa on August 2, 1862. He attended elementary school in the nation's capital and high school in Smith's Falls, Ontario before completing his formal education at Stanstead College in Québec's Eastern Townships.

Scott dreamed of studying medicine at McGill University, but bowed to financial constraints. Instead, in December of 1879, he accepted a job as a clerk in the federal Department of Indian Affairs, as it was then known. Sir John A. Macdonald himself, after a personal interview, proffered the position. "Approved," the Prime Minister scribbled. "Employ Mr. Scott at $1.50."

With these auspicious beginnings, Scott embarked on a career that was spent entirely in Indian Affairs. Before his retirement in 1932, he would climb to the highest non-elected position in the department, that of deputy superintendent general.

Scott's government career provided him with the inspiration for his highly respected "Indian" poems, many of which fit the eminent poet and author Margaret Atwood's description of "condensed tragedies."

Although he became an acclaimed author, renowned for his stark poems about Indians, loggers and other inhabitants of the Canadian North, Duncan Campbell Scott never dreamt of becoming a poet when he was a teenager. Deeply interested in music and an accomplished pianist, he only began composing poetry after he met the poet Archibald Lampman, who arrived in Ottawa in 1883.

The two men were both working as humble, ill-paid civil service clerks when they first met, probably at a meeting of the Literary and Scientific Society. Recognizing that they were kindred spirits who shared a love of poetry and the Canadian wilderness, they soon became close friends. They would remain so until Lampman's untimely death in 1899 at the age of 37.

Encouraged by Lampman to try his hand at poetry and prose, Scott soon discovered that he had a talent for both. In 1887, one of his stories was accepted by the prestigious American periodical *Scribner's* magazine, which published his second poem in 1888. The following two decades saw his work published frequently in Canadian and American magazines and newspapers.

Scott privately published his first volume of poetry, *The Magic House and Other Poems*, in 1893. This was followed three years later by *In the Village of Viger*, a collection of sketches of French-Canadian life. Although two later anthologies, *The Witching of Empire* (1923) and *The Circle of Affection* (1947) contained many well-crafted stories about Indians and traders, Scott preferred to write poetry, finding that it was more manageable when he was a full-time government official.

In the early 1900s, this capable administrator rose swiftly up the hierarchy of Indian Affairs while also publishing a volume of his own work every six or so years, and co-editing a series of biographies, *The Makers of Canada*.

Practically every summer before he rose to the top of Indian Affairs, Scott journeyed to isolated native settlements to inspect his charges. On one trip, in 1906, he travelled by canoe as far north as James Bay to negotiate treaties with the Indians of north-western Ontario.

As an administrator, Scott was committed to a ruthless policy of assimilation, which required that traditional native religious rites be banned, and that native children be separated from their families and placed in residential schools. As a sensitive poet, however, he came to display great sympathy for the plight of the Indian struggling to deal with forced "progression" into "civilization."

This is well illustrated in a poem entitled *A Scene at Lake Manitou*. Written in 1933, one year after Scott retired from Indian Affairs, it focuses on the thoughts and feelings of a Native woman who is caught between the Indian and white cultures, and attempts to forge a new way of life combining elements from both.

Scott was married twice. His first wife, whom he married in 1894, was Belle Botsford, a strong-minded Bostonian and professional violinist. They had one child, a cherished daughter, Elizabeth, who died in 1907. To commemorate her death, Scott wrote a single poem, *The Closed Door*, but he was so grief- stricken that he could not bring himself to write another line of poetry or fiction for four years.

Belle Scott died in 1929, and two years after her death Scott, by now 69, married 27-year-old Elise Aylen, a fellow poet and a member of Ottawa's establishment. It proved to be a happy union.

The work that Scott produced in the 1930s and 1940s testified to his happiness for according to the late author, Sandra Gwyn, it was as good as anything he had ever written. He not only produced his own poetry and prose during these years, he also continued to edit editions of Lampman's poetry because Scott was determined to keep his friend's literary reputation alive.

During the last years of his life, Duncan Campbell Scott developed a rich friendship with E.K. Brown, a young scholar-critic, who, in his well-known study *On Canadian Poetry*, ranked his friend among Canada's major poets.

In a portrait that he limned of Scott, Brown recalled a long conversation the two men had in Scott's home at 108 Lisgar Street (since demolished to make way for a post office) in 1942. With the landscapes of Emily Carr, David Milne, and the Group of Seven looking down, Scott spoke of his arduous canoe trips in remote parts of Québec and of the changes that had occurred in human nature in the past 50 years. Scott's voice, reported Brown, was that of an old man but what it said reflected not old age but "exquisite" maturity.

The internationally recognized literary figure and onetime government mandarin was 85 when he died.

MADGE MACBETH
BROADCASTER AND LITERARY FIGURE

(1878-1965)

———◼———

" She knows everybody, and has always known everybody—which is not too difficult in Ottawa... But she has everybody sized up, and that is quite a trick. I think she looks at everybody as a character in a potential novel..."

So wrote *Saturday Night* editor B. K. Sandwell when reminiscing about Madge Macbeth, the noted Canadian author, cultural nationalist and long-time Ottawa resident, who died at her Wilbrod Street home on September 20, 1965.

Although she lived in Ottawa for many years, Madge Macbeth was born in Philadelphia, Pennsylvania. According to Peggy Kelly in *Framing Our Past*, Macbeth's birth date ranges from 1878 to 1883. The official register of births in the Philadelphia Municipal Archives discloses, however, that she was born on November 6, 1878 to Elizabeth Maffit and H.H. Lyons, of Philadelphia.

Madge was no stranger to privilege in her youth as she grew up in Maryland among relatives she described as "Southern gentlefolk" and "aristocrats." Her maternal grandmother, whose example she would emulate, was Adelaide Clayland Maffit, one of the first professional woman journalists in the United States, a feminist and a friend and supporter of Susan B. Anthony, the renowned American feminist and abolitionist.

As befitted a young American growing up in privileged circumstances in the 1880s, Madge was educated at home by a governess and then in "exclusive private schools." One of these was a finishing school, Hellmuth College, located in London, Ontario. She enrolled at Hellmuth in the autumn of 1891 after travelling from her southern home in "an old fashioned coach complete with red plush, smelly kerosene lamps and mounds of cinders." At the time she made this memorable trip she was 12 years old.

Since Hellmuth placed a great deal of emphasis on deportment, Madge learned at an early age how to enter and leave a room and how to greet and be greeted by visitors, lessons that would stand her in good stead years later when she circulated among Ottawa's political and social elites. At Hellmuth, she also acquired some journalism skills editing the school paper, *The Union Jack*. By her own admission, she was steeped in ignorance about type faces, cuts or make-up, but her job was to get a paper published and she succeeded in doing just that.

After graduating from Hellmuth, Madge Macbeth made a "pleasurable debut," as she phrased it, in Baltimore. A brief career as a mandolist and vaudeville actress was followed, in 1901, by marriage to London-born Charlie Macbeth, a graduate in engineering from the University of Toronto. The young couple lived for two years in Detroit, and then moved to Ottawa after Charlie Macbeth was offered a post in the Georgian Bay Ship Canal project.

Madge Macbeth loved Ottawa from the moment she stepped onto the platform of the Grand Trunk Railway station. Her early years in the nation's capital were difficult ones, however, largely because of the untimely death of her husband from tuberculosis. Left with two fatherless young boys, Madge Macbeth suddenly woke up to the fact that she would have to make a living to support herself and her sons.

When she was jolted into this realization—in the opening years of the twentieth century—the opportunities open to "ladies" to make a living were extremely limited. They ranged from operating a refined boarding house, working as a governess or a teacher, or, in Ottawa, holding down a civil service position. Since Madge Macbeth didn't seem to fit into any of these niches, she took up freelance writing. "I had to buy boots for the boys and there was only one way I could make a living—write."

Success crowned Madge Macbeth's initial efforts to sell stories, but then disaster loomed. For an entire year she was unable to market a single piece. Faced by the proverbial wolf at the door, Macbeth sought the advice of a highly respected journalist and author of the day, Marjorie MacMurchy. This proved to a wise move for MacMurchy provided not only encouragement but also sound tips.

Armed with good advice and determination, Madge Macbeth set out to become a successful freelance writer. Over a long career she would produce some 20 novels, as well as articles, travel literature, drama, short stories, poetry, memoirs and speeches. In fact, when she was 84, in 1963, she published her twentieth novel, *Volcano*.

The upper class Canadian, American and British circles in which Macbeth circulated were a frequent source of ideas and subject matter for her articles and novels. Between 1943 and 1945, for example, she wrote several articles on diplomats' wives for the glossy Canadian magazine *Mayfair*. One of these was a profile of Princess Juliana of the Netherlands who spent the Second World War years in the nation's capital.

Using her firsthand knowledge of Ottawa's political and social elites, Madge Macbeth wrote two satirical novels, *The Land of Afternoon* (1924) and *The Kinder Bees* (1935), employing the pseudonym Gilbert Knox. *The Land of Afternoon* caused an uproar in the national capital when it became obvious to many readers that the novel was inspired by the family life of Canadian Prime Minister Arthur Meighen and his wife Jessie.

In addition to being a prolific writer, Madge Macbeth was a fervent Canadian nationalist. She subscribed fully to the cultural nationalist goal of the CBC, established in 1936, and in her interviews and speeches she urged Canadian writers to write about Canada, its peoples, culture and values. She was as good as her word, writing numerous novels that were set in Canada and addressed Canadian issues.

Macbeth found time not only to defend and promote Canadian literature but also to become a leading member of the Canadian Authors Association (CAA), one of many cultural organizations founded in the 1920s. She was a natural leader, serving as national president for three years (1939-1941). Indeed, she enjoyed the distinction of being not only the first female national president of the CAA but also the only national president to be elected three times in 51 years (1921-1972).

Macbeth was also active on the local theatre scene—acting, writing and directing plays for many years. As a result of her work in this area she served as president of the Ottawa Drama League, now the Ottawa Little Theatre, in 1915.

When talented, hard-working Madge Macbeth died in 1965, the *Ottawa Citizen* described her as "one of Canada's best known authors." To this it could also have added "productive and versatile."

IRENE SPRY

ECONOMIST, HISTORIAN AND SELF-STYLED HERETIC

(1907–1998)

———■———

While flying from Ottawa to Toronto, University of Ottawa professor Duncan Cameron had the good fortune to sit beside the late Charles Ritchie, the well-known and erudite Canadian diarist and diplomat.

On learning that Cameron knew economist, historian and Ottawa resident Irene Spry, Ritchie blurted out, "Isn't she the most intelligent person you have ever met? She is the most intelligent person I have met. I'll do anything to avoid an argument with her."

Formidable intellect and humanity best sum up Irene Mary Spry, who was born on August 28, 1907 in Standerton, the Transvaal, South Africa, the daughter of Amelia Bagshaw Johnstone and Evan E. Biss. Her father was a senior colonial official in the educational field; his career took him from Africa to India and back to Africa.

After the outbreak of the First World War in 1914, Irene and her siblings went to live with their aunt in England. There, she obtained her early education and the first of her post-secondary degrees, a B.A. from Cambridge, where she read economics and developed her lifelong creed that all ideas have to be justified on first principles, and that you can take nothing on faith or authority. She and other Cambridge undergraduates who shared these views styled themselves the heretics.

From Cambridge, Irene went to Bryn Mawr College in Pennsylvania to study for her Masters in Social Research. While a graduate student in Philadelphia she came to appreciate the importance of first-hand knowledge to scholarship, working in a factory to learn about industry. "We pasted little bits of rubber on large bits of rubber, and only after many enquiries was it revealed to me we were making rubber boots," she once recalled.

Equipped with her newly minted Masters degree, Irene accepted a position as lecturer in the Department of Political Economy at the University of Toronto in 1929. During her years in Toronto (1929-1938), she began to research and to write in the field of economics, working closely with Harold Innis, the department's rising star. While in Toronto, she also expressed her labour sympathies and deep interest in social causes by becoming a founding member of the League for Social Reconstruction, which paved the way for the Cooperative Commonwealth Federation.

Marriage to the late Graham Spry, a celebrated proponent of public broadcasting, was followed by a move to England in 1938. With the outbreak of the

Second World War, however, Irene returned to Canada. The births of her three children, Robin, Richard and Elizabeth (Lib), interrupted her academic career, but nevertheless during the war she worked for the YWCA as an economic advisor and as an economist for the Wartime Prices and Trade Board (later the Commodity Prices Stabilization Board).

When Graham Spry was appointed Agent-General for the Saskatchewan government in Britain after the war, Irene joined her husband in London, where she helped to establish Saskatchewan House. The six-floor central London building that was to become Saskatchewan House and the family home was bomb-damaged and riddled with dry rot when the Sprys moved into it, but thanks to Irene's finds in street markets, it soon became a beautifully refurbished Georgian house. As such, it welcomed hundreds of friends and Saskatchewan exiles before the Sprys' departure for Canada in 1967.

While she was in London in the 1950s, Irene Spry became actively involved in the international women's movement, serving as the representative of the Federated Women's Institutes of Canada (FWIC) to the Associated Country Women of the World (ACWW). In this capacity, she became chair of the ACWW's executive committee and general purposes committee in 1959, and in 1968, the organization's deputy world president. She travelled around the world on behalf of the ACWW, visiting many of the 65 countries that boasted member societies and meeting rural women and homemakers.

Irene Spry returned to scholarly research and writing during her years in London. A major project was launched at the request of the Saskatchewan government, which required her to locate documents relating to the British scientific expedition into Rupert's Land led by wealthy Irish landowner, John Palliser, from 1857 to 1859. Her search led her to archives, libraries and private homes throughout the British Isles and inspired a lifelong interest in Palliser and western Canadian history. The result was several books and numerous articles based on research conducted in the United States, Canada and even New Zealand.

While pursuing John Palliser's tracks, Irene Spry had occasion to drive across the Canadian prairies and through the Rockies, accompanied by her daughter Lib and Lib's grandmother. One particular gravel trail—almost perpendicular—along which the car bumped, struck terror in Lib, who begged her mother, then in her sixties, to let her drive. Irene's response, delivered through gritted teeth, was, "If we're going to be killed, I want to be the one to do it."

After Graham Spry's retirement, the Sprys returned to Canada, where Irene resumed her formal academic career, first at the University of Saskatchewan and then, in 1968, at the University of Ottawa. Although she officially retired in 1973, she continued to teach courses in the university's Department of Economics until the early 1980s. In fact, she gave lectures in Canadian economic history as recently as 1995, three years before her death and two years after being made an officer of the Order of Canada, one of many honours and awards she received during her lifetime.

Although she was a self-styled heretic, Irene Spry was never a mere iconoclast. She was fiercely committed to various ideals and institutions. She believed passionately in public broadcasting and did not take kindly to criticism of the Canadian Broadcasting Corporation. As someone who espoused social democratic principles, she also loved Saskatchewan and what the CCF, and later the New Democratic Party, stood for in that province.

After a life crammed with work, play, love, passion and action, Irene Spry died on December 16, 1998 in her own home in Ottawa. She departed peacefully, knowing that a book that she had been working on for 20 years, *From the Hunt to the Homestead*, would be co-published by the University of Alberta and University of Calgary Presses.

VICTOR TOLGESY
SCULPTOR, TEACHER, VISUAL ARTS ACTIVIST AND WRITER
(1928–1980)

I t's not what the first-time visitor to Ottawa's City Hall expects to see: a large, majestic-looking horse gazing down from the northeast corner of the balcony that overlooks the spacious lobby and the entrance to Jean Pigott Hall.

Made of laminated plywood and entitled "The Acrobat's Rocking Horse Set Free," this captivating sculpture was created by Victor Tolgesy, one of Ottawa's best-known artists and a leading Canadian sculptor.

It should come as no surprise that this piece was partly inspired by a beloved rocking horse that the artist played with as a child. In fact, when envisaging this work, Victor Tolgesy wrote in a journal he kept, "It is going to be somewhat like the rocking-horse I once had, but also like horses on a merry-go-round. More than anything else, though, it will be a spiritual kin to horses on Russian icons."

That this fairy tale-like sculpture was partly influenced by certain Russian icons is not surprising because Victor Tolgesy was born and raised in Eastern Europe. He was born on August 26, 1928 in Miskolc, Hungary, the son of Victor and Gabriella Tolgyesy (for professional reasons, the artist spelt his name Tolgesy). His father was a high-ranking officer in the Hungarian gendarmerie, "a military man with a benign temperament...in possession of a military bearing, a chest full of medals and a passion for crossword puzzles," wrote his son in *Acrobatics*, a largely autobiographical work.

Interestingly, no one in Tolgesy's family had artistic leanings. According to the sculptor, "None of them displayed any tendency towards more adventurous forms of existence except perhaps one distant relative, who one day decided to seek his fortune in the New World..."

The artist, his one sibling (a brother) and his parents would eventually put down roots in the New World, but not before enduring the deprivations of wartime Hungary and postwar Germany. As Communism advanced westward from the USSR, they became refugees. In 1945, shortly before the Russian army entered Budapest, which had been their home, the Tolgyesy family fled that city, eventually ending up in Munich, Germany.

Until his departure for Canada, camps in and around Munich would be Victor Tolgesy's home. It was in these makeshift surroundings that the young man completed his high school education and began fashioning small woodcarvings.

In 1951, Victor Tolgesy and his parents, but not his brother (he came later), immigrated to Canada, where they settled in Ottawa. After arriving in the nation's capital, the artist found full-time employment in an office. He also took art lessons at the Ottawa School of Art. Apart from this instruction and four to five months spent at the École des Beaux Arts in Montreal, he was self-taught.

These early years in Canada saw Victor Tolgesy devote practically all his free time to sculpting. A watershed year was 1957, when sensing that he needed to better understand his European heritage, he returned to the continent of his birth, declaring, "Now, on this trip to Europe, I expect to find or discover something that will lead me in the right direction."

The sculptor spent six months soaking up art in galleries and museums throughout Europe. Then, armed with a Canada Council grant, he travelled to Denmark to study woodcarving under a well-known Danish wood carver. One of the fruits of this period was a wooden fish that the artist carved and exhibited at the 1957 World's Fair in Brussels. This sculpture is now owned by the National Gallery of Canada.

In Denmark, Victor Tolgesy met his future wife, Grethe Jensen. They would marry the following year and have two children, Michael and Tina. The family would make their home, which included Tolgesy's studio, in Britannia overlooking the Ottawa River.

The years between 1958, when the sculptor returned to Canada, and 1974, when he produced the City Hall horse, were years of artistic self-discovery; the artist experimented in several different materials and sculpted a wide variety of subjects.

In the early 1960s, when employed by a company that undertook church renovations, he carved crucifixes, alter screens and stations of the cross. But he also sculpted abstract geometric metal sculptures. These ribbons of steel, for which he became well-known in Canada, would be his trademark until about 1974 when he completely changed direction.

Turning his back on cleanly designed abstract sculpture, Victor Tolgesy began creating figurative pieces, mainly in laminated plywood and papier mâché. In complete contrast to his earlier work, they reflected what he described as a "deliberate involvement with humanity" and an art based on "the impulses of the heart."

Reminding mankind of its humanity in the midst of overwhelming dehumanizing influences had now become his overriding goal as an artist.

A celebrated example of a sculpture produced in this phase is "Acrobat's Rocking Horse Set Free." Another is "McClintock's Dream," a large, brightly coloured papier mâché piece that was completed in 1978 for the City of Ottawa, and that is suspended in the Byward Market building.

In addition to working on his sculptures, Tolgesy taught part-time for 20 years at the Ottawa School of Art, where he became highly respected for his teaching ability and noted for his gentle humour.

He also played a prominent role in the Ottawa visual arts community, encouraging fellow artists and helping to mount major exhibitions of local work. A blockbuster show was Visual Arts Ottawa's first large exhibition, staged at Lansdowne Park in June of 1975. According to well-known local artist, Jerry Grey, Victor Tolgesy was among the local art figures who "worked like dogs to pull it off."

Victor Tolgesy's reputation was such that in 1987 the City of Ottawa and the Council for the Arts in Ottawa inaugurated the Victor Tolgesy Arts Award to recognize the achievements of residents who have made an outstanding contribution to enriching the city's cultural life.

Explaining why the award was named after the sculptor, CAO's executive director, Peter Honeywell says, "The Victor Tolgesy Arts Award was established to recognize Victor's passion for his art and generosity of spirit for working with other artists. He worked during a time of limited opportunities for Ottawa artists, continually experimenting with his own art and encouraging others."

Victor Tolgesy was only 51 when he died of cancer on January 6, 1980 in Ottawa. To mark the 25th anniversary of his death, a retrospective exhibition of his work is planned to take place at the Karsh-Masson Gallery from December 9, 2005 to January 22, 2006.

ENGINEERS

Engineers employed in the building of the Rideau Waterway were the first members of their profession to arrive in what is now Ottawa. Members of the military, whose names have long since been forgotten, they were charged with mapping a route for the 120-mile plus waterway, designing canal locks, dams and water basins and dredging channels.

Only later in the century did some some celebrated engineers settle in Ottawa and then they were involved principally with railways. One of these was Thomas Coltrin Keefer, who wrote *The Philosophy of Railroads*, a stirring plea for the expansion of Canadian railways. He moved to Ottawa in 1864, two years before the first City of Ottawa department of engineers was set up. An even more illustrious engineer described in this book was Sir Sandford Fleming, who settled in the capital in 1869 when he was involved with the Intercolonial Railway. Although not nearly as well-known as Sir Sandford, Sir Collingwood Schreiber merited inclusion in this collection because he was another outstanding railway engineer who made Ottawa his home.

THOMAS COLTRIN KEEFER
ENGINEER, RAILWAY PROMOTER,
BUSINESSMAN AND AUTHOR
(1821–1915)

When Thomas Coltrin Keefer died in Ottawa on January 7, 1915, the capital lost the designer of its long-delayed waterworks system and Canada its foremost hydraulic engineer and railway promoter.

A half-brother of the renowned structural engineer, Samuel Keefer, Thomas Keefer was born in the frontier settlement of Thorold, Upper Canada (Ontario) on November 4, 1821, to George Keefer and his second wife, Jane Emory, née McBride.

George Keefer was a Loyalist, who settled in the Niagara district in 1790. He fared well in his new home, establishing a variety of businesses and amassing considerable wealth. In an age when men usually out-lived their wives, this entrepreneur, magistrate and 1812 veteran married four times, siring 15 children by his first two wives. When he died in 1858, two of his 10 sons, Thomas and Samuel, were well-known in the province.

In the course of pursuing his many business interests, George Keefer became active in the Welland Canal project, whose moving spirit was William Hamilton Merritt. Keefer's association with the canal promoter would launch young Thomas on his career as a hydraulics engineer.

After graduating in 1838 from Upper Canada College, an elite residential school for boys in Toronto, Thomas Keefer began working as an apprentice engineer on the Erie Canal. In those days engineering or "practical schools" were almost non-existent and so Keefer toiled essentially as a navvy on the canal, then regarded as the leading project on the continent for training engineers.

In 1840, the young man returned to Canada and, through his family connections, obtained a job as assistant engineer on the Welland Canal. Five years later, thanks to W.H. Merritt, commissioner of works in the Baldwin-Lafontaine government. Keefer was appointed chief engineer of the Ottawa River project, in charge of timber slides and canals for the entire Ottawa Valley. This was his first assignment as a full-fledged engineer.

Three years into the job, Keefer was fired. "I was dismissed from this position...with flattering acknowledgements of my services—ostensibly on the ground that an Engineer was no longer required, but really on the demand of Two Members of Parliament, on whom the Government depended for their majority—because I had reported against the Chats Canal, a work which was soon abandoned after about half a million of dollars of expenditure."

Keefer, it appears, opposed construction, believing that engineering was a profession or should become one with appropriate standards and ethics. Once again Merritt intervened, and through his good offices Keefer obtained a job surveying the rapids of the St. Lawrence River. In the period of unemployment that followed this assignment, he put his trenchant pen to good use writing two essays that would catapult him into celebrity ranks.

With the publication of *The Philosophy of Railroads* in 1849 and *Canals of Canada* in 1850, he became the best-known engineer in the Province of Canada. Published first in 1849 at the behest of the Montreal and Lachine Railroad, *The Philosophy of Railroads* compares the lamentable state of transportation in Canada with that of the U.S. and makes an eloquent, stirring appeal for the expansion of Canadian railways.

As the engineer later wrote, "The Preface was sufficiently youthful and startling to secure first attention to the subject, and was a truthful if 'high-faluting' description of a Canadian winter without railways."

Keefer was not content merely to write and talk about railways. He was eager to build one, but when he was denied the opportunity he turned his hand to designing and overseeing the construction of Montreal's municipal waterworks. This assignment, which consumed most of his time between 1852 and 1856, launched him on a new and important phase of his career: the designing of municipal waterworks in cities across British North America.

One of these cities was Ottawa, where Keefer completed his third municipal waterworks in 1874. He had been asked as early as 1859 to design a waterworks and sewage system for the city, but when he submitted an imaginative plan city council turned it down. A decade later, a civic committee recommended to council that the engineer be appointed to build a waterworks at a cost not to exceed $300,000, but city fathers, demonstrating a remarkable interest in thrift, ignored the recommendation.

Not until 1872, following two major conflagrations, did city council finally give the go-ahead for a system of waterworks designed by Keefer. When completed, the $1 million massive stone waterworks plant, located at the foot of the Pooley Bridge, was described by a visiting Englishman as the finest he had seen on the continent.

On October 28, 1874, 14 years after Thomas Keefer drew up his initial plan for a municipal waterworks, Ottawans were able to draw water from taps. No longer would they have to obtain it from puncheons that had been loaded onto horse-drawn drays.

Keefer meanwhile had begun planning the prestigious residential suburb known as Rockcliffe Park. In 1848, he had married Elizabeth McKay, daughter of the Honourable Thomas McKay, the Rideau Canal contractor, one of Bytown's wealthiest landowners and industrialists and the owner of a large estate in what is now called Rockcliffe. Following the death of his father-in-law, Keefer took on the task of managing the McKay fortune and, in 1864, he moved his family from Toronto to Rockcliffe.

Using his civil engineering skills, Keefer set out to plan a picturesque suburb, using for this purpose a portion of the McKay estate known as "McKay's Bush." In seeking to create a community that would retain the area's rural and scenic character, he provided for oversize lots and parkland and banned industry, business and non-residential use.

Thomas Keefer's growing reputation led to his appointment as one of the Canadian commissioners to the First International Exhibition in London in 1851. He was appointed Canadian commissioner to the Paris Exhibition in 1878, the same year he was awarded le legion d'honneur and created a Companion of the Order of St. Michael and St. George by Queen Victoria.

Perhaps even more important, Thomas Keefer became the founding president of the Canadian Society of Civil Engineers in 1887. As such, he presided over the founding of an organization dedicated to promoting professionalism in engineering. His dedication to this cause was not limited to Canada since the year after the Canadian society's founding, he was elected the first Canadian president of the American Society of Civil Engineers.

During his latter years, Thomas Keefer devoted much of his time to managing the McKay estate and to advancing engineering as a profession. In addition, he served as president of the Ottawa City Passenger Railway (incorporated in 1866 with Keefer as the major shareholder), whose horse-drawn cars connected Rockcliffe and New Edinburgh with central Ottawa. Paradoxically this great apostle of progress was reluctant to modernize the operation with the result that Ottawa issued a franchise for a rival electric street railway in 1890. In 1894, his valuable company was bought out by Thomas Ahearn and Warren Soper.

When he died in 1915 at his Rockcliffe Manor House, the *Ottawa Citizen* described Thomas Keefer as one of Canada's "Grand Old Men." The description couldn't have been more apt.

SIR SANDFORD FLEMING

CIVIL ENGINEER, INVENTOR, SCIENTIST AND ADVENTURER

(1827–1915)

———————■———————

"It is no exaggeration to say that Canada has never had a citizen more distinguished or better known to the world than the late Sir Sandford Fleming," proclaimed *The Globe* following the engineer's death on July 22, 1915.

The inventor of Standard Time, chief engineer of the Intercolonial and Canadian Pacific Railways, scientist, promoter, the designer of Canada's first postage stamp and onetime Ottawa resident, Sandford Fleming was born in Kirkaldy, Scotland on January 7, 1827 to Andrew and Elizabeth Fleming. Kirkaldy, a beachhead of the Industrial Revolution, was in the midst of a building boom when Fleming was born. Since his father was a building contractor, who benefited from the frenetic building activity, the future engineer and his seven siblings were raised in comfortable circumstances.

From his father, Sandford Fleming inherited drafting and mechanical skills, which he put to good use at school, excelling in mathematics and attracting widespread attention with his drawing. Among those who took notice of these skills was John Sang, one of Kirkaldy's leading surveyors and engineers.

When he was 14, Fleming left school and apprenticed to Sang, who was then involved with the new railway lines from Edinburgh to Perth and Perth to Dundee. Fleming thus became associated with the nascent steam railway revolution: a remarkable piece of good luck as far as the advancement of his career was concerned.

Although the Industrial Revolution had been good to him, Andrew Fleming decided that the family's future prospects would be better in British North America. His Scottish common sense, however, cautioned him to test the waters first before uprooting his whole family and transplanting them to the New World accordingly, in 1845, he arranged for Sandford and his older brother, David, to try their luck in Canada. If they fared well, the rest of the family would follow, which they did in 1847.

After a storm-tossed sea voyage and an overland journey by paddle-wheel steamer, river barge, steamer and horse cart, the two young men arrived in Peterborough, Canada West, the home of their father's cousin, Dr. John Hutchison. David, a trained carpenter, soon found employment, but since Peterborough had no opportunities for an apprentice engineer, Sandford headed for Toronto, armed with letters of introduction to influential citizens.

Unfortunately, Fleming had trouble finding a job. Only after an exhaustive search did he succeed, and all because of a good word from Dr. Hutchison to a government surveyor. Thanks to his relative's intervention, young Fleming obtained a position as a journeyman surveyor. However, before he could certify as a surveyor, in 1849, he had to generate income. To do this he prepared maps of Peterborough, Coburg, Hamilton and Toronto.

The Toronto map was published in 1851, the same year that Fleming designed Canada's first stamp, the Three-Penny Beaver. In employing the beaver in his design, Sandford Fleming became the first designer in the world to depart from the established practice of using a royal head or some official emblem in his stamp design.

In June of 1849, Fleming participated in the founding, in Toronto, of the Canadian Institute, intended to be a professional society of surveyors, architects and engineers. When it failed in its mission, he helped to convert it into a broadly based scientific society. Over the years it would help to advance his various interests, such as universal Standard Time, and become one of his preferred sounding boards.

Fleming's railway career began in 1852 when he became an assistant engineer on the Ontario, Simcoe and Huron Union Railway, then being built between Toronto and Georgian Bay. He became chief engineer of its successor, the Northern Railway of Canada, in 1855. With the permission of the railway's board, Fleming also became involved in other projects, one being Toronto's Palace of Industry, which he helped to design.

In 1863, while he was still living in Toronto, the Canadian government appointed him chief surveyor of the first section of a proposed railway from Québec City to Halifax and Saint John. He subsequently became chief engineer of the road, the Intercolonial Railway, a position that he would fill until 1876.

In order to work more closely with the federal government, Fleming brought his family from Halifax to Ottawa in 1869, where he purchased a Daly Avenue Italianate mansion that he later named "Winterholme." Since he had to shuttle back and forth between the nation's capital and the Maritimes on business, he also purchased a summer home in Halifax.

Despite the burden of his Intercolonial duties, Fleming accepted the position of chief engineer of the Pacific railway in 1871. In this capacity he organized major surveys across the prairies and through the Rocky Mountains. He proposed that the railway be constructed along a northerly route and although his recommendation was not accepted, his extensive surveys of various routes, such as the Kicking Horse Pass, greatly facilitated later Canadian railway construction.

Notwithstanding all his work on the Pacific railway project, Fleming was summarily dismissed in 1880 by the minister of railways and canals, Sir Charles Tupper, who believed that Fleming had become a political liability because of his outspoken stance on the Pacific scheme. The engineer nevertheless continued to have an impact on the railway, even after it was taken over by a private syndicate in 1880. In fact, in that famous photograph of Donald Smith driving the last spike of the Canadian Pacific Railway in November of 1885, Fleming is the imposing central figure with the beard and top hat.

Steam and electricity, Fleming contended, were the "twin agencies of civilization," but only on land, not at sea. In 1879, he began promoting the linking of the trans-Canada telegraph system with a cable that crossed the Pacific Ocean. His dream was finally realized in 1902 when a cable from Vancouver to Australia and New Zealand was completed.

On his travels, Fleming was impressed by the confusion that reigned in the measurement of time, both in North America and Europe. This led to his becoming a tireless advocate of a suitable world system of keeping time. In his role of promoter, he was instrumental in convening the International Prime Meridian Conference in Washington (1884), where delegates adopted the system of International Standard Time that is still used today.

As a Presbyterian, Fleming had a lifelong faith in knowledge. It was therefore fitting that he was appointed, in December of 1879, chancellor of Queen's College at Kingston, where his great friend George Grant was principal. Fleming remained in this post until his death.

Fleming was noted for being not only a talented engineer and a visionary, but also for being a man of great charm and vigour. He also earned a reputation for generosity. For example, when he turned 70 in 1897, he commemorated this milestone by sending £3 in sterling to 111 people.

In his later years Sandford Fleming devoted much of his time to church and business affairs, and to giving expert advice to business and industry. After a lifetime during which he was showered with honours, he died in Halifax in 1915. He was survived by three sons and two daughters, his wife, Ann Jane (Jean) (née Hall) having predeceased him in 1888.

SIR COLLINGWOOD SCHREIBER

OUTSTANDING RAILWAY ENGINEER AND CIVIL SERVANT

(1831–1918)

———■———

"His participation in the national dream stands as his most significant contribution to the country's economic and regional development," observes Sean Gouglas in his *Dictionary of Canadian Biography* profile of Collingwood Schreiber.

Less eloquent but equally applicable is the verdict of the *Ottawa Journal*, which, in March 1918, claimed the noted engineer, civil servant and Ottawa resident was "instrumental in creating sensible railway systems in Canada..."

Collingwood Schreiber, who devoted his career to railway development in Canada, was born December 14, 1831 in Bradwell-on-Sea, Essex, England, the fourth son of the Reverend Thomas Schreiber and Sarah Bingham. His mother boasted a distinguished lineage. Her father was Rear Admiral Joseph Bingham. Her mother, Sarah, was the daughter of Vice-Admiral Sir William Parker whose wife, Jane Collingwood was the sister of Lord Cuthbert Collingwood, second in command under Nelson at the Battle of Trafalgar in 1805.

Collingwood Schreiber did not enter the British navy, however. Instead, he trained as an engineer and surveyor. In 1852, when he was 21, he immigrated to Toronto, Canada West with the rest of his family.

For a man whose destiny would be linked with railways, this was an exciting and significant time to arrive in British North America, for in 1852 the Grand Trunk Railway of Canada was formally incorporated to build a railway from Toronto to Montreal. This would be the first major line to be constructed in British North America, where railway building was still very much in its infancy.

After his arrival in this country, Schreiber obtained an engineering position with the small Toronto and Hamilton Railway. In 1856, the year of his marriage to Caroline MacLean (who died in 1892), he left the firm to enter private practice with Sandford Fleming (later Sir Sandford Fleming). Schreiber remained in private practice until 1860 when he went to work as assistant superintending engineer of construction for the Northern Railway, which became part of the northern division of the Grand Trunk.

Collingwood Schreiber's first government appointment occurred in 1864 when he accepted an invitation to assist in the construction of railways in Nova Scotia. Initially, he served as part-time divisional engineer on the intercolonial railway project and assisted in the building of the Eastern Extension Railway to Pictou. He then became full-time sectional engineer for the Intercolonial Railway (October 1, 1868), by which time it had become a federal undertaking with Fleming as engineer-in-chief. At the end of 1871, the young man accepted the position of district engineer for the Intercolonial at Amherst.

Even at this young age, claims Gouglas, Schreiber based all his engineering decisions on engineering considerations alone, not on political factors. In the construction of the Intercolonial, for example, he backed Fleming when that engineer decided that the railway should adopt the Folly Lake route through the Cobequid Mountains in Nova Scotia rather than the Madison Brook route, which would only serve to please local interests.

Schreiber's practice of basing his engineering decisions solely on engineering considerations was characteristic of the man, and is no more vividly illustrated than by an interview that took place between Sir John A. Macdonald and Schreiber. As reported later by an amused Agnes Macdonald, who had witnessed it, her husband had tried to impress upon the engineer the importance of giving a government contract for cement to a friend and supporter of the Conservative party. "I want cement that will stick," said Schreiber. Sir John, mindful of votes, continued arguing persuasively that the output was much the same in all good works—the difference to be considered was the owners. "I want cement that will stick" was the only reply. "All right, Schreiber, have it your own way," laughed Sir John.

In 1873, Collingwood Schreiber became chief engineer of all government railways in operation. Although impressed by the immense engineering difficulties that such an undertaking promised, he subsequently dedicated himself to realizing Macdonald's dream of linking Canada by a transcontinental railway. In this he would join CPR giant William C. Van Horne, who became a close friend.

Schreiber replaced Fleming as chief engineer of the Canadian Pacific Railway in June 1880, and the following month he became general manager of all government railways in operation. When serving in this position he worked out of the newly established Department of Railways and Canals in Ottawa. In describing this job, Schreiber defined his duties as seeing that Canada's "roads are operated with economy, and the business conducted with dispatch."

Upon the retirement of Toussaint Trudeau as deputy minister of Railways and Canals, Schreiber assumed that position (1892). When the engineering responsibilities for railways and canals were combined in one position, this glutton for work took on that job as well. He retained his positions as deputy minister and chief engineer when the Liberals, under Wilfrid Laurier, swept into office in 1896.

Collingwood Schreiber was 73 in 1905, when he was succeeded as deputy minister and chief engineer by Matthew Joseph Butler, who allowed his predecessor to take on the newly created government post of consulting engineer on the western or Grand Trunk Pacific division of the National Transcontinental Railway.

Despite his age, Schreiber's celebrated stamina remained undiminished. He illustrated this in 1913, when he undertook an inspection tour of the Grand Trunk Pacific that included the crossing of a 214-mile gap by three small boats and a buggy. Sir Charles Tupper stated in his memoirs, published in 1914, that in his entire career he had "never met an individual gifted with so great a love of, or capacity for, work."

Collingwood Schreiber, who was made a Knight Commander of the Order of St. Micheal and St. George in 1916, took an active interest in government railway policy until his death from cancer at Elmsleigh, his Ottawa home, on March 23, 1918. He was survived by his second wife, Julia Maud, whom he had married in 1898, and three married daughters.

ENTREPRENEURS

From its infancy up until the First World War, Ottawa's entrepreneurs were to be found chiefly among the lumberers, many of whom hailed originally from the United States. Some of these timber barons, notably John Rudolphus Booth, didn't confine themselves to creating a lumber empire. They also branched into ancillary enterprises such a railways and ships. But there were also home-grown entrepreneurs. Into this category fall men like William Wylie, the man who spearheaded the founding of the highly successful Ottawa Car Company, Thomas Ahearn, an inventor who was involved in major electrification projects across Canada, and Cecil Morrison, the co-founder of Morrison Lamothe Bakery.

HAMNETT KIRKES PINHEY
BUSINESSMAN, BLOCKADE RUNNER,
AUTHOR AND POLITICIAN

(1784–1857)

▬

H e had wealth, culture and a good education. Yet despite all these assets Hamnett Kirkes Pinhey decided, in 1819, to exchange his comfortable home in cosmopolitan Georgian London for one in the wilderness of

March Township, now part of the City of Ottawa. Why he opted for this exchange is one of those paradoxes of human nature that will probably never be fully explained.

The future landed gentleman and community leader was born on December 11, 1784 in Plymouth, England, the son of William Pinhey and Mary Townley. Historian Roger Hall speculates that the name Pinhey is probably Portuguese and that possibly Hamnett was descended from merchants involved in the Anglo-Portuguese trade. In any event, by the time he was born, his family was well established in England and owned a sizeable estate in Devon.

Following his family's move to London, Pinhey was educated at Christ's Hospital school for boys (the celebrated Blue Coat school), which he entered in 1792 and left in 1799. While still very young, he went into trade, becoming first a prosperous merchant and then a produce-broker who traded on the Continent, using his own vessels.

Fluent in French and German, Pinhey successfully ran the French blockade during the Napoleonic Wars, carrying British government dispatches to the King of Prussia. The intrepid produce broker did so, knowing full well that "his personal safety was much endangered," which, of course, claims author Harry Walker, it was. For this commendable national service, Pinhey was publicly thanked by George III.

In 1812, Hamnett Pinhey married Mary Anne Tasker, the daughter of a London merchant and exporter. They would have two sons and two daughters.

Two years after his marriage, Pinhey linked up with Henry Crossley to form a ship and insurance brokers' partnership. The business proved extremely successful in its European trade until a fall out between the partners led to its failure and three years of litigation between them.

In 1819, Hamnett Pinhey officially retired from business and began to consider other possibilities. That December, he petitioned Colonial Secretary Lord Bathurst for a land grant in Upper Canada. After reporting that he had recently retired "with a small independent fortune," Pinhey declared that he intended to "found a commercial establishment in the back-settlements of His Majesty's Possessions in Canada" provided that he could acquire a grant of 1,500 to 2,000 acres "on the Banks of the Utawa." Lord Bathurst authorized the grant, but neither its size nor location was spelled out when Pinhey departed in 1820 for Upper Canada on a reconnaissance mission.

Writing to a friend in London, Pinhey explained why he wanted to settle in Canada and why his chosen location was the Ottawa River. "About a hundred and twenty miles up the river on the Upper Canadian side, a military settlement was about to be formed. In anticipation of finding the settlers there more polished than can in general be found in a new agricultural settlement, I felt a penchant to enroll myself as one among them..."

Pinhey and his clerk, Henry Edwards, set out for Canada on the *Lord Exmouth* in April of 1820. Thirty-five days out of Plymouth the ship docked at Québec, from whence the two men made their way to Montreal by steam boat. After learning in Montreal there was land available in March Township, they set off for Upper Canada, travelling by ferry, crude stage coach, "dug-out," (hollowed out of a tree trunk), and foot.

Once arrived at his property, which overlooked the scenic Ottawa River and what is now called Pinhey's Point, the retired businessman began building a 1 1/2 storey log cottage covered in clapboarding. Named Horaceville, after his eldest son, it would be expanded in stages, the last one being completed in 1849. By that time, it had become a fine stone house that projected Pinhey's social and political aspirations.

Pinhey's estate, which spanned 2,000 acres and comprised several buildings including a stone church, St. Mary's, was only one of several large properties in the area. For the most part, the others had been established after the War of 1812 by former army and naval officers, who, like Pinhey, thought of themselves as a Tory elite bound together by breeding, education and background.

In the summer of 1821, Pinhey brought his wife and children to this part of the world. Accompanying them was a large assortment of personal possessions that included more than 50 trunks containing china, jewellery and furniture.

Hamnett Pinhey quickly transformed himself into an enterprising gentleman farmer, but one with business acumen and experience. As such, he soon became the fledgling community's banker, financial adviser and leading luminary.

By 1827, with only 80 acres under cultivation, Pinhey was able to report, "I am not making a fortune but an estate. In truth I never see any money but my own." Still, he and his family managed to live well, employ a large number of servants, entertain lavishly and travel.

In addition to dabbling in real estate, Pinhey involved himself in a number of development schemes and local philanthropies. The former included road companies, agricultural societies and, not surprisingly, railways; like so many others, Pinhey had caught the railway-building mania.

A Tory, he also plunged into politics, winning a by-election in 1832 for Carleton County. After being unseated the following year because of irregularities, he took up journalism, which he would engage in for the next two decades. Under a variety of pen names, he churned out essays, and verse and letters for the *Bytown Gazette*, the *Aylmer Times*, and the *Ottawa and Rideau Advertiser*.

In these pieces, Pinhey reveals himself as an eloquent Tory prepared to heap scorn on reformers, radicals and prospective or real rebels. In fact, he was one of the most vocal and influential opponents of the provincial government's promotion of tax-supported primary education for everybody. Like his fellow Tories, he feared a revolution among the farming class should farmers and their families become better educated.

Pinhey also filled various patronage appointments. He became a member of the legislative council in 1847, and served as local reeve and warden of Dalhousie District Council and Carleton County Council.

Hamnett Kirkes Pinhey died on March 3, 1857 in Dunrobin and was buried in the graveyard of the church he had built, St. Mary's. Horaceville, his prized estate, remained in family hands until 1971, when it was sold by one of the heirs of Ruth Pinhey to the Mississippi Valley Conservation Authority. Today, it is owned and operated by the City of Ottawa, which maintains the manor house as a museum, assisted by the Pinhey's Point Foundation.

HENRY FRANKLIN BRONSON

PIONEER LUMBERMAN

(1817–1889)

———■———

He was said to be the one man who grasped the feasibility of harnessing the foaming and furious falls of the Ottawa River to drive sawn lumber, the foundation of the all-important sawn timber industry that began in

Ottawa in 1848. Henry Franklin Bronson was this farsighted lumbering pioneer, and, like so many of Ottawa's lumber barons, he was an American by birth.

Henry Bronson was born in the town of Moreau in Saratoga County, New York on February 24, 1817 to Alvah Bronson and Sarah Tinker. Of mixed Scottish and Welsh descent, the Bronsons had settled early in New England, scattering widely throughout the northern states. According to *A Cyclopedia of Canadian Biography*, the family distinguished itself by its enterprise and intelligence, producing several notable figures, including the Honourable Greene C. Bronson of the New York bench.

Young Bronson spent his youth in Queensbury in Warren County, New York where he lived with the family of John Harris, one of the area's leading farmers and a pioneering lumberman. Bronson completed his education at Poultney Academy in Vermont where, a "reliable source" claimed that he earned a reputation for being "an apt scholar in agricultural sciences." However, he soon showed "a preference for woodland foraging, predestined as he was to become a great marauder of pine forests."

Bronson took the first step in this direction when he entered into a partnership with his friend John Harris, who, in 1840, acquired extensive tracts of pine in northern New York State, and erected mills on one of the upper Hudson River lakes. Harris accepted Bronson as a partner because he had been profoundly impressed by the integrity, resolute will, sound constitution and capacity for hard work demonstrated by the younger man. Harris's faith was not misplaced for the association proved to be a highly successful and long-lasting one, continuing for 22 years.

After the stock of pine on the Upper Hudson had become severely depleted, Henry Bronson decided to sniff out lumbering possibilities in Canada. Accordingly, in the summer of 1848, he set out for the Ottawa Valley, travelling up the Ottawa River as far as Bytown, then on the edge of a vast timber frontier that boasted some of North America's finest pine forests.

While in Bytown, the young man took in the impressive sight of the thundering, foaming Chaudière Falls. The possibilities that it offered for motive power and the Ottawa Valley's rich supply of lumber made a strong impression on him. In fact, he decided on the spot that the Chaudière (the industrial area located on the islands in front of the falls) would be the ideal location for a sawmill. It wasn't until 1852, however, that Bronson was able to persuade his partner that the two of them should journey to Bytown to explore this idea further.

Once they arrived in Canada's future capital, Bronson and Harris urged the superintendent of the Ottawa River Works, Horace Merrill, to recommend that the Crown-owned "hydraulic lots" at the Chaudière be offered for sale to entrepreneurs who wanted to exploit the falls's water power. Their entreaties were not in vain.

In September, the lots came on the open market and Harris, Bronson and another American partner, William Coleman, bought a parcel of land on the north side of Victoria Island. For a typical lot in this tract they paid the munificent sum of $200.20 in "lawful money" of the Province of Canada.

Accompanying the purchase was the right to use sufficient water to drive "ten runs of ordinary mill stones" and to build a flume to propel their mills and carry saw logs to their property for 21 years.

Harris and Bronson reaped a further bonanza a short time later when they snapped up nearby building lots that had been made available at greatly reduced prices, thanks to a recommendation made to the Canadian government by Ottawa mayor R. W. Scott.

With the purchase of the hydraulic lots, the way was paved for the erection of a sawmill that "embodied all the modern improvements of the times," including novel iron gates manufactured to a design that Bronson had produced, and that would later be used by most other sawmills on the Ottawa River. It was a large plant, boasting 74 upright and four circular saws with provision made for an additional 70 upright saws.

In launching the so-called "American invasion" of this period (American entrepreneurs Pattee, Perley, Eddy, Booth and Dickinson followed in hot pursuit), John Harris and Henry Bronson demonstrated superb timing. For in 1854 the Province of Canada concluded a reciprocity treaty with the U.S. that permitted Canadian planks and boards to enter that country duty-free. With this sort of encouragement, the partners' fledgling company, Harris, Bronson and Coleman (later Harris and Bronson), soon began shipping large quantities of sawn lumber to the American market.

Once the first mill had been erected, Henry Bronson moved his wife, Edith (née Pierce), whom he had married in 1840, and their children to Bytown. The union produced four children, a daughter and three sons, two of whom (Erskine Henry and Walter Goodman), carried on the lumber business after their father's death.

John Harris, who retired from Harris and Bronson in 1864, never moved to Bytown, but remained in his home town, Glen Falls, New York. However, Henry Bronson remained in Bytown, managing the new company, which in 1867 became known as the Bronsons and Weston Lumber Company.

In building up the business, Bronson had to surmount "many serious obstacles that would have disheartened men of ordinary energy," but overcome them he did, creating a successful operation that helped to transform an unproductive falls into a flourishing industrial site, and a backwoods village into a prosperous city. Indeed, Bronson's success was such that he created an empire that, prior to his death, stretched from Mattawa, Ontario to New York City, and that chalked up more than one million dollars worth of business annually.

Henry Bronson did not shun active involvement in Canadian politics. After the Reciprocity Treaty was terminated in 1866, reports Robert Peter Gillis, Bronson lobbied furiously to have it restored. He also supported the provincial and federal Liberals in Eastern Ontario, arranging, for example, for his company's woods managers to serve as Liberal poll bosses in every constituency in which it did business.

In Ottawa, Henry Bronson became deeply involved in community affairs, becoming president of a flourishing girls' school, the Ottawa Ladies' College, a pillar of St. Andrew's Church and a benefactor of numerous local causes.

One recipient of his generosity was the City of Ottawa, which in 1872 undertook to build a pumping station and lay water mains. Henry Bronson gave the city the land on which the pumping station was to be built and in 1874 the construction was completed.

After being in failing health for some time, Henry Franklin Bronson died of a stroke at age 72 on December 7, 1889. Such was the affection and respect in which he was held that 207 carriages and a large number of Chaudière mill hands took part in the cortège that proceeded from his home on Concession Street, where the funeral was held, to Beechwood Cemetery, where his remains were interred in the family vault.

MOSS KENT DICKINSON

KING OF THE RIDEAU

(1822–1897)

———————■———————

In the 1850s and 1860s, when he was a force to be reckoned with in the shipping and forwarding business, Moss Kent Dickinson was dubbed by the *Ottawa Citizen* the "King of the Rideau." This noted Ottawa Valley figure was more than just an astute shipping magnate, however.

He was also an industrialist who launched several pioneer industries, a lumberer and a politician who served in both the municipal and federal arenas.

A lineal descendant of the Pilgrim Fathers who sailed on the *Mayflower*, Moss Kent Dickinson was born on June 1, 1822 in Lewis County, New York. He was the youngest son of an affluent businessman, Barnabas Dickinson. Barnabas, the son of Mollie Little and Lemuel Dickinson, a Massachusetts land owner and farmer, had left his ancestral home in Hatfield in 1806 for the frontier lands of upper New York State. There, he had settled first in Lowville, then in neighbouring Denmark, where Moss was born.

Moss Kent Dickinson, named after a family friend, lawyer Moss Kent, became a resident of Canada in 1828 after his father Barnabas moved his family to the bustling St. Lawrence River town of Cornwall to start a stage coach service. When he was of school age, the youngster returned to Lewis County to attend Lowville Academy where his namesake had been a trustee.

After completing his formal education at age 16, young Dickinson opted for a job with Hiram Norton, a family friend and business associate. The enterprising Norton had helped Barnabas and his older brother, Horace, to launch a profitable Canadian stage coach service, and had gone on to operate his own stage coach services and to serve in the Upper Canada legislature. When Norton left Canada under a cloud in 1838, Moss accompanied him to Illinois to work as his clerk.

Returning to Canada two years later, the future entrepreneur landed a job as a postal and customs clerk in Prescott, working for his brother-in-law, Alpheus Jones. Dickinson, however, had long been fascinated by ships; in 1844, he realized his dream of establishing his own shipping and forwarding business.

The resulting line grew so rapidly that by 1850 it boasted some 16 steamers and 60 barges. These plied the water from Oswego, New York to Québec and from Ottawa to Whitehall at the foot of Lake Champlain, reaping a good return for their owner.

In fact, at the pinnacle of its success the so-called "Dickinson Line" monopolized the shipping business in the St. Lawrence-Ottawa-Rideau River Triangle and Lake Champlain.

But Moss also entertained other ambitions. In 1850, he entered into a partnership with Vermont-born John M. Currier, who had left for Canada in 1837 to seek his fortune in the lumber business. The two partners subsequently rented and operated Thomas McKay's mills at Rideau Falls, thereby becoming the first entrepreneurs in the Ottawa Valley to ship sawn lumber to the American market.

Having become trail blazers in the lumber business, Dickinson and his partner proceeded in 1859 to build an imposing limestone grist mill, now owned by the Rideau Valley Conservation Authority. Lauded as one of the best examples of 19th-century grist mill architecture in Canada, it is located in the town of Manotick, Ontario, which Dickinson named in 1864 after the Ojibway word for "island in the river." Today an historic landmark, the mill became an integral part of Dickinson's shipping and milling empire on the Rideau.

The four-storey building, which has changed hands several times over the years, has always been distinguished by its impressive appearance. When it was built, however, it was also marked by its advanced technology, for according to authors Harry and Olive Walker, Dickinson and Currier were among the first to jettison the "over shot" water wheel for the new turbine water wheels that lie flat on the river's bed-rock.

Unfortunately, in 1861, a year after the building's gala opening, tragedy struck. When John Currier conducted his elegantly dressed bride of two months, Ann Crosby, on an inspection tour of the premises, her billowing skirt caught in a revolving turbine shaft. Before the machinery could be stopped, she was flung against a post and killed. Grief-stricken, Currier left the partnership in 1863 and moved to New Edinburgh, where he established new enterprises and proceeded to build what would eventually become the residence of Canada's prime ministers, 24 Sussex Drive.

Dickinson also suffered a grievous loss in these years: his beloved wife, Elizabeth, died in 1861, five months after giving birth to a daughter, Elizabeth. All told, Moss and Elizabeth had six children, one of whom, George, later took over the mill's operation.

Although he founded the village of Manotick, Dickinson and his children did not reside there until 1870. After relocating from Ottawa, they moved into a spacious frame house that Moss had built in 1867 directly across from the grist mill.

When the family lived in Ottawa, in the 1860s, Moss Kent Dickinson tried his hand at politics. He took the plunge in 1864 when Ottawa was hovering on the brink of bankruptcy as a result of its involvement with the Bytown and Prescott Railway, and the fallout from a depression. A candidate of the newly established Municipal Reform Association of Ottawa, Dickinson became mayor in January 1864. He occupied this office until 1866, accrediting himself well, but relieved when his term was up and he was able once again to devote all of his energy to his business enterprises.

A devout Conservative and an active supporter of Sir John A. Macdonald, Dickinson capped his political career by carrying the county of Russell for the Conservative party in the general election of 1882. Five years later, in the federal election of 1887, his Manotick home once again served as a Conservative campaign headquarters, but this time Dickinson was not a contestant.

Moss Kent Dickinson died on July 19, 1897 after a lengthy illness. In its relatively short obituary, the *Ottawa Citizen* described him as "one of the pioneers of this district" and "a widely known and respected man." Now that we realize that Moss Dickinson played an outstanding role in his community for close to 50 years, this can hardly be described as fulsome praise.

JOHN RUDOLPHUS BOOTH

LUMBER MAGNATE AND ENTREPRENEUR

(1827–1925)

———■———

I
f ever there was an Ottawa celebrity who personified the "Alger hero," it was John Rudolphus Booth. Born into a humble farm family on April 5, 1827, he succeeded by dint of hard work, determination and resourcefulness in becoming the

multimillionaire "dean of Canadian lumbermen" and one of Canada's most successful entrepreneurs.

The son of Irish immigrants John Booth and Eleanor Rooney (Rawley), J.R., as he was familiarly known, was born in a stone farmhouse in Shefford County, near what would become the village of Waterloo in Québec's Eastern Townships. As a youth, he spent his summers chopping wood and his winters acquiring the rudiments of a formal education at the local county school.

The continuous and seemingly futile round of hard toil in which family members and neighbours engaged made a deep impression on young Booth. When he was 21, therefore, he left the farm, determined to make a better life elsewhere. His first destination was Vermont where for several years he worked as an apprentice carpenter, building bridges for the Vermont Central Railway. In 1853, during this first phase of his career, he married Rosalinda Cooke, who also hailed from the Eastern Townships.

The years spent working in Vermont and the Eastern Townships persuaded Booth that his hands alone would not make him rich. Hoping to better his prospects, he set off in 1854 with his wife and infant daughter for Bytown, then a lusty, brawling lumber town with a rapidly growing sawn timber industry. A town on the move, Bytown would be incorporated as the City of Ottawa the following year, but not until 1857 would it be chosen as the capital of the Province of Canada.

Before laying the foundations of his own lumber empire, Booth helped to build Andrew Leamy's sawmill three miles north of Hull. As a result of his industry and resourcefulness, the future lumber baron was soon appointed mill manager. He served in this capacity for one year, during which time he and his wife occupied their evenings splitting shingles to sell to local residents.

Asked by his employer to open another mill, Booth decided that he would be his own boss. He rented a sawmill near the Chaudière Falls on the Ottawa River and began producing shingles. When the building was destroyed by fire a few months later (the first of many setbacks he experienced during his career), Booth rented another mill on a one-year lease. His operation was so profitable that at the end of the first year, his landlord attempted to double the rent. Booth responded by building his own mill at the Chaudière Falls.

J.R.'s first big coup came in 1859 when he undercut his competitors for the contract to supply lumber for the Parliament buildings, then under construction. Having secured the contract, he went in search of a suitable stand of timber, which he found near Constance Creek, west of Britannia. With characteristic shrewdness, he used money-saving horses rather than the traditional, more cumbersome oxen employed by his competitors to haul timber from the forest. Booth's innovative move paid off. He realized a substantial profit from the venture and his name became widely known in the lumber industry.

With his profit from the Parliament Hill contract, Booth financed a substantial sawmill at the Chaudière Falls. By 1865, his annual output of 8 million board feet made him the third largest producer at this location. Twenty-five years later, his mill complex at the Chaudière boasted the highest daily output in the world.

It was essential that Booth have a guaranteed source of timber for his rapacious mills. He therefore outbid competing timber barons for a vast timber limit of 250 square miles once owned by another lumber magnate, John M. Egan. Eventually Booth, the astute industrialist, would amass the largest timber limits in Canada and become the largest manufacturer of lumber for both the American and British markets.

John Rudolphus Booth's reach extended beyond timber. He also sank money into railways with a view to obtaining low-cost access to the New England timber market. He became the major shareholder of the 135-mile long Canada Atlantic Railway, planned as a route from Ottawa to the Vermont Central Railway. And while the Canada Atlantic was being built, he incorporated the Ottawa, Arnprior and Renfrew, and the Ottawa and Parry Sound Railways to serve as feeder lines to the Canada Atlantic Railway. In addition, he bought control of the Parry Sound Colonization Railway, which together with the recently incorporated Ottawa and Parry Sound Railway, furnished him with a route from Ottawa to Georgian Bay and an additional 265-mile feeder line for his Canada Atlantic.

The enterprising Booth added value to this railway by entering the grain trade. With the goal of providing prompt delivery of his grain, he organized the Canada Atlantic Transit Company, a steamship company that carried grain and packaged goods in five large freighters on the Upper Great Lakes. And he built elevators at Depot Harbour near Parry Sound and at Coteau-Landing, Duluth and Milwaukee.

J.R. Booth was renowned for his iron will and his hard work. He worked well into his nineties, remaining in full possession of his mental faculties and continuing to astound people with his astuteness. He played an active role in all aspects of his business, yet at the same time, he was a very private man. Although he fully involved his nephew, J.R.B. Coleman, in his lumber operations, he didn't inform him that he operated a fleet of ships on the Upper Great Lakes.

Outside of work Booth indulged in his one hidden passion: flowers. Throughout his life, he made a practice of seeing every flower show that he could. Recognizing this, in the 1930s the Central Experimental Farm named a yellow exhibition chrysanthemum that it had developed after him.

An unassuming man, who dressed in unfashionable clothes, Booth normally shunned publicity like the plague. He even refused to attend the wedding of his granddaughter, Lois Frances Booth, who, in 1924, married Prince Erik of Denmark. The event was probably the most celebrated society wedding ever to take place in Ottawa.

Despite his aversion to publicity, Booth's influence made itself felt throughout the business and political circles of the nation's capital as well as in such local institutions as St. Luke's Hospital, to which he contributed generously. The *Ottawa Citizen* alluded to the industrialist's and philanthropist's unique standing in the early days of the capital when, on December 10, 1925, the day after his death, it described him as the "emperor of the woods" and "monarch of the Upper Ottawa."

Booth himself, however, would have probably preferred the description provided by former Prime Minister, Rt. Honourable Arthur Meighen. Speaking at the time of J.R.'s death, Meighen said, "His vision, his unerring judgment, his quiet generosity, and his sincerity made him an outstanding gentleman among his fellows. The words of admiration and goodwill one hears from all those who worked for and with him are a tribute as well to his character as to the eminence of his place among Canadians."

ALEXANDER SMITH WOODBURN

PHILANTHROPIST AND NEWSPAPER FOUNDER

(1830–1904)

◄■

"In Mr. Woodburn the strength of the north of Ireland blood, which showed itself in his fine physical presence as well as in his character, was associated with a moderation, tact and obliging good nature which made him an element of kindliness wherever he was found. We are sure he will be missed and regretted in the business world of this city, where he was to the last a familiar figure, very specially regretted in the circles which were familiar with his philanthropic work..."

So wrote The *Evening Journal* in 1904 on the death of Alexander Smith Woodburn, a pillar of good works in his community and one of Ottawa's most prominent and respected citizens.

The third child and first son of James and Martha (née Mayne) Woodburn, Alexander Woodburn was born on November 13, 1830, in Garvagh, County Derry, Ireland. He spent the first decade of his life in Northern Ireland. Then, in 1841, he, his parents and four siblings immigrated to Canada where they settled first on the Mountain Road in Hull Township, then near Green's Creek, Gloucester Township.

When the Woodburns arrived, Hull Township was so sparsely settled that neighbours were often separated by a mile of dense forest. To reach the nearest town, the family had to travel eight miles to Hull. Alexander Woodburn would later recall that only one family in 20 in those early days received a letter or newspaper. Therefore, loaned copies of the *Belfast Newsletter* and the *Northern Whig* were eagerly read by all the settlers among whom they circulated.

After homesteading for a year or two in Hull Township, the Woodburns moved to Gloucester where they took up farming. However, young Alexander decided not to remain on the family farm. When he was approximately 13 he moved to Ottawa to learn the printer's trade under Dawson Kerr, publisher of the *Orange Lily*, a small weekly newspaper that was launched in 1849. After serving his apprenticeship, Alexander worked as foreman for Alexander Gibb, proprietor of the longer established *Bytown Gazette*.

Woodburn worked for Alexander Gibb for several years before leaving him to go into partnership with John George Bell. The partnership was successful; the two men built a prosperous printing and book-binding establishment on Elgin Street. that employed between 60 and 80 people.

Woodburn carried on the business alone after his partner died in 1874. Financial problems arose, however, after the death of his son, Sydney, a young man of great promise who had joined his father in running the printing establishment. Still, the business appeared outwardly prosperous when Alexander founded the *Ottawa Evening Journal* on December 10, 1885 with the aim of creating an independent, fair and honest newspaper.

Unfortunately, the *Journal* swallowed up so much money in its start-up years that Woodburn's financial problems multiplied. In 1891, when his printing business was failing, he was forced to sell his remaining interest in the Journal to P.D. Ross, to whom he had sold a half share in 1886. Shortly after divesting himself of his remaining interest in the *Journal*, Woodburn joined the staff of the paper's printing company.

An editorial published after his death lauded Woodburn for accepting "the business reverses which came upon him with a dignity, a serene and quiet dignity, which showed neither complaint nor loss of mental or moral grip." As portrayed by the article, Woodburn spared no "toil to avert the crash," working from early morning to almost midnight to retain his printing business.

A man of commanding presence, who stood over six feet, Alexander Woodburn also figured prominently in the affairs of his community. One of his many interests was the military in which he played an active role, helping to found the Ottawa Field Battery in 1855 when the Crimean War was making news headlines and new militia units were sprouting across Canada. In later years he served in the Fenian Raids of 1866 and 1870, and was instrumental in founding the Fenian Raid Veterans' Association in Ottawa.

Although not enamoured of politics, Alexander Woodburn nevertheless represented Wellington Ward on city council in 1871. After his one-year stint on the council he never again showed any interest in re-entering the municipal arena.

Once out of politics, this public-spirited citizen focused his energy and time on philanthropic work, for which he became best-known. A lifelong desire to alleviate suffering and assist those in distress inspired Alexander Woodburn to serve on the board of the County of Carleton General Protestant

Hospital. As chairman of the board, he strove hard to advance the hospital's interests, in the process earning a reputation as one of the institution's mainstays.

While serving on the hospital's board, Woodburn came to recognize the need for a home for aged and infirm men. This led him to spearhead the establishment of the Protestant Home for the Aged, an institution dedicated to caring for elderly men. As the hard-working secretary of the home, Woodburn earned the plaudits of the *Journal*, which claimed that the institution's "successful accomplishment of its mission" was "due almost entirely to his labours."

Woodburn's deep interest in philanthropy expressed itself in his contributions to two other organizations. A teetotaller, he helped to organize the Sons of Temperance Lodge in Ottawa. He was also instrumental in founding the Irish Protestant Benevolent Society.

Alexander Woodburn's non-business interests embraced more than philanthropic work and the militia. He was extremely active in the Methodist church, a director of Ottawa Ladies' College (a flourishing girls' school), and a prominent player in the agricultural fair movement. In fact, for many years he was the secretary-treasurer of the County of Carleton Exhibition Association.

When he passed away on March 31, 1904, at his Henderson Avenue home, there were few men in Ottawa better known than public-spirited, kind Alexander Woodburn. He was survived by his wife, Hannah Mills, whom he had married in 1862, and four daughters.

THOMAS AHEARN

ELECTRICAL ENGINEER, INVENTOR AND PROMOTER

(1855–1938)

H e has been described as one of Ottawa's true local heroes, a "professor of electrical energy" and "one of the big men of Canada."

The subject of these accolades, Thomas Ahearn, was born on June 24, 1855 on Duke Street in Lebreton Flats to John Ahearn, a blacksmith, and his wife Norah (née Power), natives of Waterford, Ireland.

In 1870, after abruptly leaving the Ottawa College, Ahearn approached the local office of the Montreal Telegraph Company offering to deliver messages in exchange for the chance to learn telegraphy. Within six months he had become so skillful at receiving and sending telegraph messages he was promoted to operator-messenger.

The young man's mastery of this relatively new marvel of communication served him well for it helped to subtly, but effectively, give him a wider sense of the world beyond "backwoods" Ottawa. At age 19, he set off to seek his fortune in bustling New York City, where he found employment with the Western Union Telegraph Company as a telegrapher.

At the height of his illustrious career, Thomas Ahearn observed of these early years, "I started as a messenger boy and am proud of it. I tried to do my work well. I never loitered by the way; I did not have time as I needed every minute to perfect myself in telegraphy. The boy who loiters on the way when sent on an errand too often remains the errand boy throughout life."

After a two-year stint in the Big Apple, Ahearn returned to Ottawa as chief operator for the Montreal Telegraph Company. From henceforth he would make his home in Ottawa, the launching pad for many of his most outstanding achievements and the city that, in the words of journalist Keith Woolhouse, he would shape "to a degree that few have managed."

The inventive and ambitious young man created a sensation in 1879 when he devised a primitive telephone system based upon a *Scientific American* article that described Alexander Graham Bell's pioneering efforts. Using two-handmade sets fashioned from cigar boxes, and tapping into an existing Ottawa to Pembroke telegraph line, Ahearn made the capital's first long-distance phone call. Having made newspaper headlines, he then sold his newfangled phone for $16 to settle a hotel bill.

Ahearn's unauthorized use of Graham Bell's patented technique raised the spector of legal action. However, the threat was never realized. In 1880, in one of life's small ironies, Ahearn was appointed manager of Bell Telephone Company's first local office. While employed by Bell, he was responsible for the installation of a company switchboard in the Parliament buildings, where he made friends with members of the Press Gallery and MPs, including Sir John A. Macdonald and Sir Wilfrid Laurier, who became a close friend.

In 1881, Thomas Ahearn teamed up with Warren Soper, former manager of the Dominion Telegraph Company's local office and a boyhood friend, to form a partnership known as Ahearn & Soper, Electrical Engineers. Before its demise as a result of Soper's death in 1924, this dynamic partnership would be responsible for constructing and equipping a wide range of electrical projects across Canada.

An early undertaking involved the installation of 165 arc lamps in the capital by the Ottawa Electric Light Company, established by Ahearn and Soper in 1882. On the strength of the street-lighting contract awarded to the company in 1885, the two men immediately set out to build a simple power station to generate the electricity necessary to light the lamps.

Two years later, Ahearn & Soper formed the Chaudière Electric Company in Hull to furnish power to businesses in that community. It was merged with the Ottawa Electric Light Company in 1895, at which time the partnership bought out their main competitor, Standard Electric, thereby obtaining a virtual monopoly on electricity services in the nation's capital.

One of the firm's bigger coups occurred in 1890 when it obtained the franchise to operate electric streetcars in Ottawa. At the time, Ottawa's transportation system consisted of only sleighs, omnibuses and horse-drawn cars that were heated in wintertime by tiny coal stoves.

Horsepower met its first big challenge in 1891 when the Ottawa Electric Railway Company, headed by Thomas Ahearn, began operating a fleet of horseless streetcars manufactured by a St. Catherines, Ontario plant. The first line opened on June 25. Five cars carrying invited guests rumbled at a leisurely pace from the new car barns on Albert Street to the Lansdowne Park exhibition grounds. When Ahearn installed heaters in three of the company's cars in 1893, they became the world's first electrically-heated streetcars.

Hitherto, electric street-railways had been considered impractical for Canada as it was thought that wintertime snow would pose operational problems. Ahearn successfully met this challenge by purchasing two American sweepers to keep the track clear. Later sweepers would be produced by the Ottawa Car Company.

Not content with proving that electric streetcars could be operated successfully in a northern climate, Ahearn invented and patented an electric cooking range. This range enabled the inventor to chalk up still another world first when he used it to cook a dinner at Ottawa's Windsor Hotel on August 28, 1892. In describing this headline-making repast, *The Ottawa Journal* referred to it as "cooking by the agency of chained lightning."

Ahearn once again made headlines when he, Soper and William Wylie, an Ottawa carriage and wagon builder, incorporated the Ottawa Car Company in September of 1893. Within two decades, the company would become Canada's pre-eminent streetcar builder.

A public-spirited man, Ahearn also left his mark on the national scene. On July 1, 1927, the Diamond Jubilee of Confederation, he successfully organized a coast-to-coast radio broadcast that Governor General Lord Willingdon declared, "had done more to create a national spirit in Canada than any other movement." Following this success, Ahearn was made a member of His Majesty's Privy Council for Canada.

Meanwhile, the versatile pioneer had taken on the chairmanship of the Federal District Commission, the forerunner of the National Capital Commission. During his five-year tenure, which ended in February of 1932, the Commission accomplished more than it had in the previous 30 years. One of his many achievements, which included the development of much of Ottawa's parkway network, was the completion of the Champlain Bridge.

When Ahearn became Commission chairman, it looked as though the bridge would terminate at Bate Island because of a lack of funds. Undaunted by this financial crisis and convinced that the project was a worthy one, the chairman proceeded to borrow several thousand dollars on his own personal security. As a result, the bridge was completed.

The man known as "the Edison of Canada" died in Ottawa on June 28, 1938, having collected 11 Canadian patents and become an outstanding Canadian figure in industry, finance and business. Along the way, he had also found time to raise a family by his first wife, Lillias (Ahearn married her sister, Margaret Fleck, in 1892, four years after Lillias' death), travel around the world, and pursue his passion for driving motor cars.

WILLIAM WASHINGTON WYLIE

PIONEER STREET CAR MANUFACTURER

(1860–1921)

I t will no doubt come as a surprise to many that Ottawa was once home to an electric street car manufacturing pioneer and to the founder of a highly successful street car manufacturing company, the Ottawa Car Company.

This one-in-the-same trailblazer was William Washington Wylie, who was born in Valpariso, Chile on May 17, 1860.

Apparently, William Wylie's parents, Robert and Jane Wylie (née Ross), intended to emigrate from Scotland to the United States, but when they were en route to that promised land, their boat ran into difficulty. Rescued by a ship bound for Chile, the two Scots ended up by settling in that country instead of America.

Although he was born in Valpariso, William Wylie was educated in Paisley, Scotland, where he later apprenticed in the carriage trade. Following his apprenticeship he worked as a carriage-builder for Liverpool's tramways company, honing his skills in wooden construction techniques and acquiring some knowledge of metal working as well.

In 1881, the young man married Ellen Rennie in Paisley. Two years later, in July 1883, he set sail for Québec City on the Allan liner *Sardinia*. His wife, accompanied by their son John, followed in September of that same year on the Allan line's *Parisien*.

After working for the Grand Trunk Railway shops in Montreal, William Wylie launched his own wagon and carriage-building business in Bell's Corners, on the outskirts of Ottawa. He then moved to the capital, where he formed a partnership with Richard Shore to manufacture carriages and wagons.

After fire destroyed their Slater Street factory in 1891 and Shore left Ottawa, Wylie decided to set up on his own. Using his meagre savings, the up-and-coming entrepreneur invested in a small factory on the same site, the corner of Slater and Kent Streets. Initially, a shortage of capital made it difficult for him to keep the business operating smoothly, but then a local bank manager came to the rescue. He had such faith in the industrious, hard-headed Scot that he offered to "see him through."

William Wylie's first big breakthrough came in December of 1891 when the electrical consulting firm, Ahearn and Soper, placed an order with his company for six open wooden cars and one vestibule car. The vestibule car, which would highlight Wylie's craftsmanship, was to have a cherry wood interior that boasted fancy glass lamps and seats upholstered in the best Wilton carpet.

In July of 1892, the consulting firm's partners, Thomas Ahearn and Warren Soper, placed still another car order with William Wylie Car and Carriage manufacturers. This time, however, the cars were not intended for use by the Ottawa Electric Railway, established earlier in the year, but for the Winnipeg Street Railway.

The flurry of activity in the Kent Street factory attracted the attention of the local press. That same July, the *Ottawa Evening Journal* reported that "Mr. Wylie of Kent Street, who is now becoming famous for his cars, is having an addition built to his factory." The following month, the *Ottawa Citizen* noted that the car-builder had completed an addition to his establishment on Kent Street and was engaged in manufacturing seven cars for the Ottawa Electric Railway Company.

William Wylie's success in filling these orders attracted business from elsewhere, including the Montreal Street Railway. Soon his entire work force of "27 hands" was required to work overtime to meet the demand for new cars.

Hard on the heels of this success came a decision by some shareholders of the Ottawa Electric Railway to buy out Wylie and establish the Ottawa Car Company. The new company was incorporated on September 7, 1893. Among its major shareholders was Wylie, who held the largest number of shares, one quarter of the stock. He would remain the largest shareholder until his retirement in 1911.

At the time of the company's incorporation, Thomas Ahearn, who with Warren Soper had established the Ottawa Electric Railway, was listed as president and William Wylie as superintendent. In 1896, however, Wylie's title was changed to vice-president and managing director. Irrespective of title, William Wylie was the guiding genius of the firm, which was fast developing an enviable reputation for its electric railway cars, carriages and wagons.

No sooner was the Ottawa Car Company incorporated than new buildings were erected and the work force enlarged. Strenuous efforts were also devoted to promoting its electric street car business. As a result, company cars were soon running in Victoria, Vancouver, St. John, Halifax and Kingston.

Before he retired from the company, William Wylie savoured the pleasure of seeing it move from success to success. Under his direction, it produced the first large double truck cars for Canada, built transport wagons for use in the Boer War and produced gun carriages, limbers and ambulances, all the while manufacturing high-quality street cars. In fact, the company's street cars earned a reputation for being among the best produced on this continent.

The Ottawa Car Company was not William Wylie's sole passion, however. He was also an enthusiastic hunter and fisherman, and a charter member of the Ottawa Hunt Club and the Abitibi Fish and Game Club. When it came to recreation, though, he was perhaps best-known for being one of the first owners of an automobile in Ottawa. A motoring enthusiast, he is reported to have purchased his first car in 1899 when the car industry was still in its infancy.

William Wylie died unexpectedly of a stroke in his sixty-second year, leaving behind his widow, his son and three daughters. In the obituary that it ran the day he died, June 24, 1921, the *Ottawa Evening Journal*, lauded him as "one of the pioneer electric car manufacturers in America, a foremost resident of Ottawa, a man of outstanding business ability, an enthusiastic sportsman and a great lover of the out-of-door life."

G. CECIL MORRISON

**BUSINESSMAN, UNIVERSITY GOVERNOR
AND GOVERNMENT ADMINISTRATOR**

(1890–1979)

———■———

O n the afternoon of July 1, 1967, the centenary of Canada's
founding, thousands of people crowded onto Parliament
Hill under sunny skies to celebrate the occasion with
Queen Elizabeth, Prince Philip and other dignitaries.

There were speeches but undoubtedly the afternoon's major attraction, apart from the royal couple, was the 20-foot high, four-tier birthday cake made by the capital's largest bakery, Morrison Lamothe.

Watching each tier of the mammoth cake being unloaded from a flatcar and hoisted into position by a construction crane proved to be an emotionally charged experience for the bakery's president, 76-year-old G. Cecil Morrison. A loyal monarchist, staunch Conservative and prominent businessman, he could never have dreamed in 1915 when he co-founded a small bakery that one day he would preside over the huge enterprise that was now providing refreshments for Canada's Parliament Hill centennial celebration.

The future "happy baker," as he came to be known, was born at Low, Québec on September 22, 1890, to John and Lydia Morrison (née Brooks). Cecil Morrison's father, who farmed a 100-acre concession in Bristol Township, was of Scottish descent. His mother was the granddaughter of Caleb Brooks, who had emigrated from Massachusetts to Lower Canada in 1818 to work as a millwright for Philemon Wright, his uncle-by-marriage.

Following the practice of the day when there were no maternity hospitals, Cecil's mother had returned to her parents' home for her confinement. A month after her son's birth, however, she set out with him for her husband's farm, located four miles from Shawville, Pontiac County's political centre. The trip by horse and buggy took two whole days, reported Cecil Morrison in his autobiography, *The Life & Times of G. Cecil Morrison: The Happy Baker of Ottawa.*

Taught by his mother to read and write, young Cecil did not enter school until he was eight years of age. Like so many other country youngsters of the day, though, he never made it to high school, leaving after completing grade nine to work on the family farm.

Wresting acres from the forest was such back-breaking work that it instilled in the youngster a deep respect for Canada's pioneers. Nevertheless, he hated the drudgery and was never really happy unless he was working in the family store, run first by his grandfather and then by George Morrison, his uncle. From this venerated uncle, Cecil Morrison learned many valuable lessons, including the basic truth that in business the customer is always right.

When he was 16, Morrison's boyhood was rudely shattered by the death of his beloved uncle from pneumonia. The young man begged to be allowed to carry on the store, but when this idea was vetoed he set off for the bustling national capital with high hopes and $60 in his pocket. The year was 1908 and Ottawa, with a population of only 60,000, had the air not of a national capital but of a small provincial town.

In Ottawa, Cecil Morrison enrolled in Willis's Business College, which provided him with a good basic training in business. It also introduced him to Richard Lamothe, another country boy off the farm. The two would become good friends and later business partners and brothers-in-law.

After graduating from business college, young Morrison obtained a job with the Dominion Express Company. There, he worked 13 hours a night, from 6:00 p.m. to 7:00 a.m., six days a week and learned what would prove to a valuable lesson for the future: how to lay out delivery routes.

Employment at the express company was followed by a job at the Bank of Ottawa. The bank offered security and a good pension plan, but the pay was small and the promotions slow. Moreover, it had a rule that no one could marry until he was earning $1,000 a year. In 1915, therefore, Cecil Morrison left his teller's job to join his friend, Dick Lamothe, in founding the Standard Bread Company.

Two years later, in September of 1917, the young businessman married Margaret Jane Kelly Cotter, the daughter of John Cotter, a cabinetmaker from Belfast. The marriage produced three daughters, Jean, Margaret (Grete) and Gay, all of whom would come to play a leading role in the Ottawa community.

Meanwhile, the company Cecil Morrison had co-founded was growing. As a result, it moved in 1924 from Hilson Avenue in Nepean to Ottawa's Gladstone Avenue, where it established a new modern bakery. In the "Roaring Twenties," the post-war boom years, Standard Bread prospered, opening a branch in Montreal, initiating plans for one in Toronto, and then entering into a merger with the Lake of the Woods Milling Company's chain of bakeries.

When the Great Depression began ravaging Canada, Cecil Morrison was general manager of the large Inter-City Baking Company and a highly successful, prosperous businessman. However, all this changed in 1932 when he lost both his job and his fortune.

Luckily, employment did not escape him for long. In 1933, Morrison and Dick Lamothe took over bankrupt, down-at-the-heel Dominion Bakeries on Echo Drive. This was the beginning of Morrison Lamothe, which would grow into a baking, catering and frozen food empire.

As its president, Cecil Morrison introduced several progressive programs, including a comprehensive medical plan for company employees and their dependents, a group insurance policy, a contributory pension plan and, in the years when the company was doing well, a profit-sharing scheme.

Outside the office, Morrison contributed to the Second World War effort by serving as bread administrator for Canada under the prices and trade board. In this capacity he succeeded in obtaining the cooperation of bakers to hold the price of bread at pre-war prices.

Following the war, in 1952, the businessman helped to found Lowren Housing Company to provide accommodation for low-paid Ottawa workers and their families. The company subsequently embarked on a two-phase program to provide rental accommodation for senior citizens, a first for the city.

A member of the University of Ottawa's board of governors from 1965 to 1978, Morrison played an instrumental role in drawing up a new charter that allowed the Roman Catholic institution to become eligible for provincial grants, but at the same time retain its historic character.

In September of 1967, when he reached the age of 77, the "happy baker" turned over the Morrison Lamothe presidency to his eldest daughter, Jean Pigott. However, he continued as chairman of the board until 1975 when he was made life-time honorary chairman.

Cecil Morrison was 88 when he passed away on February 26, 1979 in his home, Bayne House, a heritage house that he and his wife had lovingly restored decades earlier.

MAYORS

Bytown held its first municipal election in 1847. Expected to be a raucous affair, it proved remarkably calm and ordered. On the other hand, the candidate predicted to win the mayoralty, John Scott, did just that, becoming Bytown's first mayor that same year.

The first mayor to head the newly created City of Ottawa was John Bower Lewis, elected in 1855. Neither he nor Scott is profiled in this section. Instead, two twentieth-century mayors have been chosen: Harold Fisher, whose most visible legacy was the Ottawa Civic Hospital, now known as the Civic Campus of the Ottawa Hospital; and feisty, colourful Charlotte Whitton, the first female mayor of a large Canadian city.

HAROLD FISHER

OTTAWA MAYOR AND LIBERAL POLITICIAN

(1877–1928)

———————◼———————

A s you enter the grounds of the Civic campus of the Ottawa Hospital from Carling Avenue, you can't help but notice a concrete statue on your left. Its male subject—a tall, distinguished-looking man with a moustache—

leans slightly forward, his right arm thrust behind his back clutching a rolled-up document. At the base of the statue is an inscription that reads, "If you would see his monument, look around you."

Hackneyed as this injunction may be, it is eminently fitting in this case, for the figure portrayed by the statue is none other than Harold Fisher, the farsighted, hard-working mayor who spearheaded the establishment of what was once known as the Ottawa Civic Hospital.

The need for a hospital, funded and run by the municipality, was driven home to Fisher during the world-wide flu epidemic of 1918, which began sweeping with tornado-like speed through the nation's capital in September of that year. At its height, it struck more than 10,000 Ottawans and, in a three-week period, ending in mid-October, it combined with pneumonia to produce some 520 deaths in the capital.

Local hospital facilities, already outdated and far from fireproof, were taxed to the limit. Indeed, the demand for hospital beds was so great that the Ottawa Public School Board and the University of Ottawa hastened to furnish space for two large emergency treatment centres. Assorted service organizations, such as The Maycourt Club and the Ottawa Day Nursery, responded by providing volunteers to care for victims.

The local hospitals' shortcomings alone would have been enough to convince Fisher of the need for a municipally financed hospital. But the case for such a hospital was also bolstered by the arguments made by the then chairman of the Ottawa Board of Health, Dr. Campbell Laidlaw. To drive his point home, he took Mayor Fisher on a tour of the County of Carleton General Protestant Hospital, the Ottawa Maternity Hospital and St. Luke's General Hospital.

After this eye-opening excursion, Harold Fisher turned to the physician and announced, "Doctor, I'm going to build your hospital for you." It was one thing to convince the mayor that a new municipally financed hospital should replace the three obsolete, privately-owned hospitals. It was another matter, however, to persuade the members of the local medical profession, all of whom did not initially share his views.

Many doctors, hospital trustees, administrators and nurses were extremely loath to see three venerable institutions, with which they had strong ties, eliminated to make way for a new hospital that would be administered by a public body, the Corporation of the City of Ottawa. To dispel these worries, a great deal of behind-the-scenes manoeuvring was required.

Fortunately the mayor, an able administrator, had finely honed political and diplomatic skills that were equal to the task. At his urging, the various professional groups and hospital trustee boards were brought together to examine the situation in exhaustive detail. The result was a unanimous decision that the City should sponsor a new hospital.

Under Harold Fisher's leadership, City Council adopted a plan to take over the assets of St. Luke's General Hospital, the County of Carleton General Protestant Hospital and the Ottawa Maternity Hospital, and to replace these with a modern institution operated by the municipality. City Council then applied to the Ontario legislature for authority to raise $1,500,000 by debentures.

To present the case for a new, municipally-administered hospital, a delegation led by Fisher journeyed to Toronto to appear before the Ontario legislature's private bills' committee. Luck was with the delegation, and in its 1919 session, the Ontario legislature passed the Ottawa Civic Hospital Act.

After the passage of the act, another major hurdle remained to be overcome: the choosing of a suitable site for the projected hospital. Not surprisingly, this excited a good deal of interest on the part of both vested interests and the general public. Finally, after much haggling and controversy, the Reid Farm site (23.496 acres bordering Carling Avenue) was chosen. The press immediately dubbed the location "Fisher's Folly" because of its perceived remoteness from the city's downtown core.

While leading the fight against the flu epidemic, Harold Fisher struck up a friendship with his future wife, Jessie Argue, then superintendent of the Lady Grey Sanatorium. They were married the following year, in 1919.

Coincidentally, this tireless champion of a new civic hospital was the son of a doctor. Harold Fisher was born on November 1, 1877 in Battleboro,

Ontario to Dr. J.H.F. Fisher and Myra N. Clemota. After graduating from public schools and Toronto's Jarvis Street Collegiate Institute, young Fisher studied at the University of Toronto and Osgoode Hall. He was admitted to the Ontario bar in 1902.

Harold Fisher began his law career with the well-known Toronto firm, Beatty and Blackstock, but in 1903 he decided to move to Ottawa and enter a law practice with Charles Murphy (later Senator Murphy). Fisher's outstanding abilities as a lawyer were officially recognized when he was made a King's Council in 1920, the year he relinquished the mayoralty.

Fisher took his first plunge into politics in 1913, when he ran for alderman for Wellington Ward and won. He served two years as an Alderman (1913-14) and two terms as a Controller (1915-16) before becoming mayor in 1917.

As mayor, observed the *Ottawa Evening Journal*, Harold Fisher "brought to the discussion and handling of the city's business a trained mind, a vigour and freshness of view, a reputation for integrity and a patient and humane course of action that made the citizens realize that a new and better era had dawned with Harold Fisher's advent at City Hall."

A lifelong Liberal, Fisher entered provincial politics in June of 1923 when he was elected as a Liberal to the Ontario legislature for West Ottawa. His popularity and practical grasp of public business were such that he succeeded in attracting the votes of many Conservatives. And no sooner was he elected than he was selected as the opposition's financial critic.

Harold Fisher served as an MLA until December of 1926 and then returned to full-time practice as a lawyer, declining "honours which less gently-disposed men would have seized with eagerness." He also served as a trustee on the board of the Ottawa Civic Hospital, having been appointed to the board on the death of A. W. Fleck in 1924 to complete that trustee's term. He remained a trustee until his death.

The highly respected politician and lawyer, avid reader and outdoorsman was only 51 when he succumbed to pneumonia on December 19, 1928. He was survived by his wife, Jessie Argue.

CHARLOTTE WHITTON

SOCIAL WORKER, AUTHOR AND POLITICIAN

(1896–1975)

W hen she was Ottawa's flamboyant mayor in the 1950s, redoubtable Charlotte Whitton had occasion to meet the Lord Mayor of London at a ceremonial function. The Lord Mayor, wearing his official robe and chain of office, looked at Charlotte, similarly attired, and asked, "If I smell your rose will you blush?" Charlotte immediately shot back, "If I pull your chain, will you flush?"

This retort is typical of those attributed to feisty, sharp-tongued Charlotte Elizabeth Hazeltyne Whitton, who has also been credited with saying, "Whatever my sex, I'm no lady," "Trust in God and She will provide", and "Whatever she does, woman must do twice as well as any man to be thought of just half as good—luckily it's not difficult."

The legendary social worker, author, feminist and politician was born on March 8, 1896 in Renfrew, Ontario, the first child of Elizabeth Langin Whitton and John Edward Whitton, who worked as a merchant and caterer for lumber companies. The couple came from markedly different backgrounds. Ontario-born John Whitton, described as both taciturn and "mischievous," was of Yorkshire Methodist stock while his wife was a Roman Catholic of Irish descent.

Charlotte was baptized into the Anglican faith as were the siblings who followed her: John, Mary (who died when only two years of age), Kathleen and Stephen. In later years this devout Anglican would observe, "My mother's a Catholic. My father was an Orangeman. Where does that leave me? Right in the Anglican Church."

The Whitton children were raised as Anglicans until 1907 when Elizabeth Whitton made the momentous decision to return to the faith in which she was raised. She was accompanied by the three surviving younger children but not Charlotte. Lottie, as she was then called, stoutly refused to attend St. Francis Xavier Roman Catholic Church. When taking this action, claim her biographers P.T. Rooke and R.L. Schnell, Charlotte early demonstrated that she was a determined individual steadfastly committed to her principles.

From an early age Charlotte Whitton excelled at school. She did so well at Renfrew Collegiate Institute that she won enough prize money to pay for a four-year university education at Queen's University. There, she again chalked up a brilliant academic record, all the while revealing a consuming passion for service. Eventually this ardour would lead to a career in social service, the budding feminist believing that this was a field in which she could best serve the feminist cause by work, accomplishment and success.

The outstanding student graduated from university in 1918 with an M.A. in philosophy, history and English. Although this designation would suggest otherwise, this was not a postgraduate degree but an honour awarded to her for her outstanding undergraduate record. Fittingly, Whitton's graduation picture bore the inscription, "She will brook no tarrying—where she comes the winds will stir."

Within a week of leaving university, the proud graduate went to work for the Toronto-based Social Service Council of Canada as assistant secretary and assistant editor of the newly founded social work journal *Social Welfare*. As assistant secretary of Canada's major voluntary social service organization, Charlotte Whitton not only handled correspondence but she also attended child welfare and charity conferences at the municipal and provincial level, and wrote articles on social policy.

New opportunities opened up in 1922 when she took up a position in Ottawa as private secretary to Liberal MP Thomas Low, later minister of Trade and Commerce. In addition to working for Low, energetic Charlotte Whitton served as honorary secretary for the fledgling Canadian Council on Child Welfare (later the Canadian Council on Child and Family Welfare), Canada's major national child welfare organization. Four years later she became the council's first full-time director; as such, she built up the council, made an invaluable contribution to social work training, and helped to standardize child welfare practice and policy across Canada.

When the Great Depression ravaged Canada, Whitton moved onto a larger stage. In 1932, she investigated employment relief in Western Canada for the R.B. Bennett government, and in 1937 she advised the National Employment Commission on how to reform the relief system.

Charlotte Whitton, however, was a pronounced social conservative. As such, she not only denounced more liberal divorce laws and criticized married women who worked, but she also opposed more liberal spending on the unemployed. In her view, only the depression's true victims—those who were normally neither dependent nor underemployed—should be entitled to federal funds.

Whitton's social work career entered a new phase altogether in 1941 when she resigned from the Canadian Council on Child Welfare (now known as the Canadian Welfare Council) to take up contract writing, consulting and lecture tours of Canada and the United States. The speaking tours thrust her further into the limelight, especially in the Unites States, where she was promoted as "Canada's Welfare Ambassador Extraordinary" and adulated by the press.

Further recognition came as a result of journalism articles and the publication of two books—*The Dawn of Ampler Life* (1943), an investigation of social security undertaken for the federal Conservative Party leader John Bracken, and *A Hundred Years A-Fellin* (1943), a history of the Ottawa Valley lumber industry. During this often overlooked period, the indefatigable Whitton championed women's equality in the workplace and politics, and completed commissioned studies on welfare administration and adoption procedures.

In 1950, Charlotte Whitton embarked on a second career, this time in municipal politics. Elected a controller on Ottawa city council in 1950, she went on to become the first female mayor of a large Canadian city in 1951. In this new role she proved herself to be both colourful and controversial.

Nevertheless, the feisty, fast-talking mayor refused to be "treed" like an old cat at election time, winning two terms in 1952 and 1954.

The venerable warrior was defeated when she attempted to win the federal riding of Ottawa West as a Progressive Conservative, but she returned as mayor in 1960 and 1962. In 1964, however, she was defeated by mayoralty candidate Don Reid.

On the eve of her defeat, Charlotte Whitton was accorded a full column plus a photo in the Sunday *New York Times*, a feat, claimed Charles Lynch, that no Canadian prime minister had been able to perform. "Her fame spanned the oceans, enlivening a world that has more than its share of dull characters," wrote the late journalist.

Whitton didn't abandon civic politics, however. She became an alderman in the 1966 election and was subsequently re-elected and remained in office until she resigned in 1972.

In her later years, Charlotte Whitton adopted as one of her final causes, that of the elderly. Fighting on their behalf, she argued for "oldster power" and railed against stereotypes in this age group, the lack of serious research on the subject and the ridiculing of the elderly in popular television comedies.

Charlotte Whitton died on January 25, 1975 after spending 24 days in the Ottawa Civic Hospital following a heart attack. After being given the first lying-in-state ceremony ever for a former mayor and a civic funeral, she was buried in Renfrew beside her dear friend Margaret Grier. In a tribute to Whitton, the *Ottawa Citizen* described her as, "A woman of contrasts, difficult to understand but well worth understanding..."

MEMBERS OF PARLIAMENT AND JUDGES

On December 10, 1859, Parliament, sitting at Quebec, voted to make Ottawa the fixed seat of government of the Province of Canada. It wasn't until June 6, 1866, however, that the first, and, as it turned out, the only session of the Parliament of the Province of Canada to meet at Ottawa, opened. The following year would see the city ("Westminster in the Wilderness") become the capital of the new Dominion of Canada.

With its confirmation as the fixed capital of first the Province of the Canada and then the Dominion of Canada, Ottawa became the second home of many parliamentarians and the first home of others. Among those who settled here permanently was Sir Richard Scott, who played a prominent role in having Ottawa selected as the permanent capital of the Province of Canada. Another parliamentarian who made Ottawa her home was Cairine Wilson, Canada's first woman senator. The outstanding jurist, Sir Lyman Duff, and Eugene Forsey, professor, labour activist and onetime senator, were other well-known figures who put down roots in the capital.

SIR RICHARD WILLIAM SCOTT

LAWYER AND POLITICIAN

(1825–1913)

——————■——————

Long-time Ottawa resident, Sir Richard Scott, has several claims to fame. Not the least of these was the role he played in Ottawa's selection as the fixed capital of the Province of Canada.

In 1857, when Scott was the city's Member of Parliament, he extolled the city's virtues in an eloquent memorial that helped to convince the Colonial Office in London that Ottawa was ideally suited to become the provincial capital. He then mounted a vigorous lobby to persuade the provincial parliament to ratify Queen Victoria's approval of this choice of site. His campaign was crowned with success on December 10, 1859 when Parliament, sitting at Québec, voted to make Ottawa the fixed seat of government of the Province of Canada.

The city's champion was born in Prescott, Upper Canada on February 24, 1825, the son of Dr. William James Scott, whose ancestors came from County Clare, Ireland, and Sarah Ann McDonell, the daughter of a loyalist, Captain Allan McDonell, who had settled in Matilda Township, Upper Canada. William Scott had served as a hospital mate in the Peninsular War before coming to Québec in 1814 and subsequently settling in Prescott, where, according to biographer Brian Clarke, he established a "large but unremunerative" practice.

Richard Scott was raised a Catholic and educated by a tutor at home. He started his apprenticeship in law in 1818 and, in 1848, after being admitted to the bar, he established a law practice in Bytown (as Ottawa was called at the time), where he also engaged in real estate and operated a sawmill.

Before long, Scott plunged into municipal politics, serving first as a councillor (1851) and then as the city's mayor (1852). When he was mayor he was horrified to learn that the Orangemen's twelfth of July parade planned to wind its way through Irish Catholic shantytowns. Determined to prevent bloodshed, he decided to ride at the head of the procession, believing that the presence of a Catholic would nip any rioting in the bud. Although the occasion was tense, Scott did succeed in defusing a riot. Still, he lost the next municipal election.

Scott was Bytown's mayor when he began a celebrated romance with Mary Heron, an accomplished singer. While attending a musical evening featuring the Herons, a well-known family of entertainers, Scott fell instantly in love with Mary, one of the singing sisters. A persistent man, he returned with a large floral bouquet for her the following night and followed the troupe back to New York, where he persuaded her to marry him. This accomplished, he brought her entire family to live in Ottawa.

As mayor, Scott came to the aid of the timber barons by helping to convince the Commissioner of Crown Lands to auction off the hydraulic and building lots on the islands adjacent to the Chaudière Falls, and to lease the water power of the channels to interested parties.

Scott would continue to represent the interests of the timber barons throughout his political career. In addition, he would become a spokesman for the interests of Roman Catholics, most notably after he was elected to the provincial legislature in the election of 1857-58.

In 1860, following consultations with the Catholic hierarchy, Scott introduced a private member's bill to extend and codify the rights of separate schools. This bill and its successor failed to obtain second reading. Undaunted, Scott pressed on with his campaign, finally succeeding in his mission in 1863.

The resulting legislation would form the constitutional basis for Ontario's separate school system after Confederation.

Richard Scott became provincial commissioner of crown lands in Edward Blake's cabinet on December 21, 1871. When occupying this portfolio he stirred up controversy by authorizing the rapid sale of northern timberlands on an unprecedented scale. In fact, in 1873, he ignited charges that he was acting on behalf of the lumber interests.

When Alexander Mackenzie formed a government in 1873, after the Pacific Scandal, he invited Scott to be the Irish Catholic representative in his cabinet. Scott obliged by resigning from the Ontario legislature and cabinet to become a minister without portfolio. He was appointed Secretary of State on January 9, 1874 and a member of the Senate two months later, on March 13.

Ontario's English-speaking Catholics lauded Scott for championing their educational rights, but on the national stage, he became best-known for the Canada Temperance Act of 1878, or the Scott Act, as it was usually called. Under this act, a petition by a quarter of the electors in a county or municipality could trigger a vote to ban the local sale of alcoholic beverages.

A teetotaller from his youth, Scott was convinced that such legislation was essential to "put down vice and crime."

Although he abstained from alcohol, Scott established a model farm in Québec, where, according to his great grandson, Ian Scott, he planted 53 different varieties of grapes. Scott was also a vegetarian, but he didn't impose his vegetarianism or his alcohol abstinence on guests. In fact, he and his wife entertained lavishly and kept a well-stocked wine cellar.

After Mackenzie's government was defeated in 1878, Scott led the Senate's Liberal opposition. He continued to gain wider recognition, becoming an elected member of the Dominion Law Society in 1879 (he practised law in Ottawa during his political career there) and receiving an LLD from the University of Ottawa in 1889.

From the late 1880s on, Scott acted as the principal intermediary between the new Liberal leader, Wilfrid Laurier, and English-speaking members of Ontario's Catholic hierarchy. Thanks to his addiction to work and his enviable knowledge of Parliament Hill, Scott became one of Laurier's most trusted colleagues.

Richard Scott was 81 before he took his first holiday. Work, claimed this strong proponent of clean living and exercise, was his "chief recreation." He stayed at his post even during the summer months when cabinet colleagues were off on vacation, keeping Laurier, who was at home in Arthabaska, up to date on business.

The Prime Minister appointed Scott Senate leader in 1902, but Scott resigned from cabinet and the leadership of the Senate six years later, believing he could no longer maintain the frenetic pace required by his duties. In recognition of his services, he was created a knight bachelor in 1909.

Although retired from the cabinet and the leadership of the Senate, Scott continued to attend Senate sessions. In fact, he last addressed the upper house the month before his death.

This "Nestor of Canadian Liberalism," as he was described, died on April 23, 1913 at his Daly Avenue home following prostate surgery. His renown was such that his funeral cortège to Ottawa's Notre Dame Cemetery was estimated to have been three-quarters of a mile long.

SIR LYMAN DUFF

DISTINGUISHED CANADIAN JURIST

(1865–1955)

H is biographer, David Ricardo Williams, described him as "Canada's most distinguished jurist." The *Ottawa Citizen* touted him as "one of the great legal minds of North America," noting that his only legal equals on this continent were Mr. Justice Brandeis and Mr. Justice Holmes of the United States Supreme Court.

Long-time Ottawa resident, Sir Lyman Poore Duff, was richly deserving of these accolades for he sat on the Supreme Court of Canada longer than any other jurist, from 1906 to 1944, serving as its Chief Justice for his last 11 years. For 27 of those years, he was also a member of the judicial committee of the Privy Council in England, then the court of final appeal for Canadian litigation.

Of Scottish lineage, Lyman Duff was born in Meaford, Ontario on January 7, 1865 to Charles Duff, a Congregational minister, and Isabella Johnson, an intellectual with a voracious appetite for books and classical literature. Her gentleness and interest in literary works had a marked influence on Duff, who, in his final years, spoke not of his father but of his mother, who died in 1902.

Thanks to his father's frequent moves from one pastorate to another, Duff spent his youth in various parts of Ontario as well as in Nova Scotia. His first formal education was obtained in a one-room school in Brooklyn, Nova Scotia. At age 10, he made the transition to a grey stone schoolhouse at Speedside, in the heart of rural Ontario. A bright child, he read Hansard regularly as well as Dickens's novels, histories of England, Shakespearean plays, and accounts of celebrated battles and soldiers.

Emulating the example of his father, who moved countless times in his career, Duff changed schools frequently in the years leading up to university. Despite the many interruptions, he remained a serious student. Indeed, by age 15 he was determined to pursue a career in law. In order to attain this goal, he entered University College, one of the constituent colleges of the University of Toronto, in 1881.

By the time he arrived at university, Duff had developed political views that mirrored those of his father, a devout Liberal. According to his biographer, Duff's lifelong Liberal sympathies would play an important role in developing his character, and influence many of his actions as a lawyer and a judge. Unlike his father, however, Duff did not become a dedicated teetotaller, vehemently opposed to the consumption of the "demon liquor." On the contrary, he became an alcoholic whose abuse of the bottle and near catastrophic binges dogged his career and almost prevented him from becoming Chief Justice.

After becoming a qualified lawyer, in 1893, Duff established a practice in Fergus, Ontario. It was short-lived because the following year he accepted an invitation from a close friend to join him in a partnership in Victoria. With his friend, Gordon Hunter, Duff established the firm of Hunter & Duff and launched his career as a busy courtroom lawyer. Within three years he had eclipsed most other litigant lawyers in the province.

The rising legal star left the partnership in 1897 to join another law firm. That same year he married Elizabeth Bird (Lizzie) and attended a Liberal Party convention as a first-time Victoria delegate. Still in his thirties, the popular jurist was elected president of the B.C. Liberal Association.

Duff reached the pinnacle of his profession in British Columbia in the opening years of the twentieth century. In December 1900, he was appointed Queen's Counsel and in 1903, a member of the team of Canadian lawyers who joined their British counterparts in appearing before the tribunal established by the United Kingdom and the United States to settle the Alaska boundary dispute. It was no doubt thanks to this last appointment that Duff was appointed to the Supreme Court of British Columbia in 1904 and, in 1906, to the Supreme Court of Canada.

His elevation to the Supreme Court of Canada led Duff to take up residence in Ottawa where in 1910, he and his wife built an imposing house on Golbourne Avenue in Sandy Hill. This would be Duff's home until shortly after Lizzie's death in 1926, when the jurist moved to Daly Avenue.

Duff served on the Supreme Court during a period when Canada was evolving from an agrarian society to a modern industrial state, and when he and the court had to wrestle with important issues concerning the meaning of the constitution. The judgments he wrote in constitutional matters are still pre-eminent today.

Initially, claims university law professor, Richard Gold, Duff took the position that the provinces and the dominion government had been granted powers separately by the United Kingdom and that these powers were mutually exclusive with little, if any, overlap. Over time, however, the jurist altered his views on the relationship between the federal and provincial governments; he finally concluded that a "certain degree of concurrent power had to be tolerated" and that the sovereign power that had rested with the imperial parliament prior to the Statute of Westminster (1931) rested with the dominion parliament after Canada's evolution into an independent state.

Lyman Poore Duff reached the most important milestone in his career when he was appointed Chief Justice of Canada on March 17, 1933. Another was made the following year when he was knighted. In the New Year's Day honours list, the Chief Justice was made a "member of the Knights Grand Cross of Our Most Distinguished Order of Saint Michael and Saint George."

Duff served as interim head of state several times and chaired several commissions before retiring from the Supreme Court in 1944. One of these commissions was assigned the task of apportioning church properties between the newly established United Church of Canada and those Presbyterian congregations that had not entered the union. Another was the Transportation Commission, appointed in 1931.

Far more controversial was his chairmanship of a one-man inquiry into the Canadian government's decision to dispatch an ill-equipped and inadequately trained expeditionary force to Hong Kong in 1941. Mackenzie King's choice of Duff, a staunch Liberal, as the Royal Commissioner almost guaranteed that the government would be exonerated for its role in the Hong Kong mission. King was not disappointed.

Much more laudable was Duff's contribution to Canadian nationhood. In 1940, he upheld the power of the federal government to abolish appeals to the Privy Council in London unilaterally, thus allowing Canada to adjudicate its affairs independently. The Privy Council agreed with the jurist, but the legislation making this possible did not come into effect until January 1, 1949.

Lyman Duff died on April 26, 1955, after being confined to the Ottawa Civic Hospital for approximately two months. He was survived by his devoted sister, Annie, who, with her sister Emma, had done so much to rehabilitate him and thereby pave the way for his appointment as Chief Justice of Canada.

SENATOR CAIRINE WILSON
FIRST LADY OF THE RED CHAMBER

(1885–1962)

———————— ■ ————————

When Cairine Wilson was born on February 4, 1885, nobody could have predicted that one day she would venture into politics in Ottawa and then become Canada's first woman senator and a dedicated humanitarian noted for her work with refugees.

Born Cairine Reay Mackay in Montreal, she was the daughter of Robert Mackay, one of this country's most powerful businessmen (he was appointed a Liberal senator in 1901), and Jane Baptist, the daughter of a lumber baron from Trois-Rivières. As befitted a member of a wealthy Scottish-Canadian family, Cairine Mackay grew up in a mansion on Sherbrooke Street West in the heart of Montreal's famous Square Mile.

In these privileged surroundings she and her seven brothers and sisters were raised on a diet of liberalism and Scottish Presbyterianism, which emphasized the duty of each Christian to manifest God's will in everything he did. The Protestant work ethic and the concept of stewardship—the belief that individuals should use their talents and any wealth they have to benefit mankind—would become driving forces in her life.

Since the gruff family patriarch was a rigorous disciplinarian, luxury for Cairine Mackay and her siblings was tempered not only by the teachings of their church but also by a very strict upbringing. Still, unlike some of her brothers, she never rebelled openly against her parents' puritanical regime or against the earnest self-denial and self-discipline that Scots Calvinism implies.

However, these influences would make for a very shy, reserved woman, albeit one with a quiet sense of humour and an abundance of warmth and compassion.

Cairine Mackay attended private girls' schools, where she excelled at her studies. In fact, she ranked first in her graduation year at Trafalgar Institute, an exclusive ladies' finishing school. Nevertheless, the future senator never attended university because, with one exception, the young women from her circle of friends did not pursue higher education.

After marrying a former Liberal MP, Norman Wilson, in 1909, Cairine Wilson moved to Rockland, Ontario, where her husband was a lumber mill manager. There, Mrs. Wilson adopted the lifestyle decreed for a woman of her circumstances—raising children (eventually she would have eight) and managing a large home.

Following the family's move to Ottawa in 1918, Cairine Wilson came to the realization that life, for her, should involve more than marriage and raising children. Accordingly, she plunged into politics, becoming joint president of the Eastern Ontario Liberal Association (1921); president of the Ottawa Liberal Women's Club; the organizing genius behind the National Federation of Liberal Women of Canada in 1928; and the chief architect of the Twentieth Century Liberal Association, an organization of young Liberals that was established in 1930. The future senator also became a conscientious worker for numerous community and national organizations, such as the Victorian Order of Nurses and the Young Women's Christian Association.

The shy, wealthy matron was thrust onto the national stage on February 15, 1930 when Prime Minister Mackenzie King, an old family friend, appointed her Canada's first female senator. Her elevation to the upper chamber came almost four months after the judicial ruling that made her appointment possible: the landmark decision of the Judicial Committee of the Imperial Privy Council that women were "qualified persons" and therefore eligible to sit in the Canadian Senate. It was the direct outcome of a determined fight waged by Judge Emily Murphy and four other feminists from Alberta, who had petitioned the Supreme Court of Canada, and then the Privy Council of Great Britain, for a ruling on Section 24 of the British North America Act.

In an editorial published two days after Cairine Wilson's elevation to the Senate, *The Ottawa Journal* pronounced the appointment an excellent one. "Mrs. Wilson," claimed the paper, then one of Ottawa's two English daily newspapers, "is the very antithesis of the short-haired female type which talks of Freud and complexes and the latest novel, and poses as being intellectual. She is of the much more appealing and competent kind who make a success of their job of taking care of a home and rearing a family before meddling with and trying to make a success of everything else."

Although she owed her appointment to Mackenzie King, the hard-working senator did not let her friendship with the Liberal leader prevent her from adopting positions opposed by him. At no time did Cairine Wilson take a more public stand against his views than on October 2, 1938, when, in her capacity as the first and only woman president of the League of Nations Society in Canada, she issued a statement attacking the Munich Agreement, which allowed Germany to occupy Czechoslovakia's Sudeten area. In condemning the accord, Senator Wilson pitted herself not only against Mr. King, but also against many other influential Liberals.

Cairine Wilson distanced herself from the values of the Canadian establishment by supporting progressive measures and by embracing the cause of refugees, many of whom were Jews fleeing Nazi Germany. When the senator took up their cause in 1938, Canada was mired in the Great Depression, and Canadians resolutely opposed large-scale immigration, fearing that it threatened the loss of more jobs.

Despite such formidable obstacles, Cairine Wilson worked tirelessly as chair of the Canadian National Committee on Refugees, a non-sectarian pressure group, to educate Canadians about the contributions talented refugees could make to Canadian society and to bring about a liberalization of Canada's highly restrictive immigration laws. She lobbied vigorously to have individual refugees admitted to this country, frequently succeeding in this endeavour while losing the battle to bring about a more humane immigration policy.

Among the many refugees that Senator Wilson assisted were highly educated anti-Nazi Germans, Austrians and Italians, who were transported from Britain to Canada in 1940 and then interned in Canadian camps. After the war many of these men became Canadian citizens, thereby providing their adopted country with one of its most remarkable pools of foreign-born talent.

The work that Cairine Wilson did on behalf of refugees proved to be the most demanding and challenging of her entire Senate career, which included a stint as chair of the Senate Committee on Immigration and Labour from 1948 to 1961. In the post-war years, she also became the first woman to be appointed to the Canadian delegation to the United Nations General Assembly (1949).

The senator died in Ottawa on March 3, 1962. Today, she is usually remembered as Canada's first female senator, but there is another title that she rightly earned and was proud to bear. To thousands of the refugees she helped, Cairine Wilson was known as "Mother of the Refugees."

SENATOR EUGENE FORSEY
SESSIONAL LECTURER, CONSTITUTIONAL AUTHORITY,
AUTHOR, SENATOR, INVETERATE LETTER WRITER

(1904–1991)

W hen a publisher in the late 1980s suggested that he write his memoirs, long-time Ottawa resident Eugene Forsey replied that he'd "sooner be sentenced to penal servitude" than embark on such an undertaking.

But then some years later the well-known Canadian relented and the result was a work modestly entitled *Life On the Fringe*.

Eugene Forsey may indeed have lived a life on the fringe, but he earned a unique place in Canadian life as a constitutional expert, critic of governments, labour leader and friend of countless prominent people. He cemented this distinction by using his formidable intellect, prodigious learning and acerbic wit to fight passionately for numerous causes, among them English literature, British parliamentary democracy, the monarchy, social justice and a united Canada.

Undoubtedly the cause closest to his heart was a united Canada. As retired journalist Edward W. Barrett once remarked, "Forsey stood on guard for Canada. He did battle for Canada—one Canada. He loved Canada."

In battling for one Canada and his other causes, the redoubtable Forsey used lecture halls, radio, TV and the floor of the Canadian Senate to expound his views. It was in a steady stream of letters to newspaper editors (the editor of *The Globe and Mail* was the principal recipient), however, that the late bilingual senator and social activist became best-known to members of the general public. From the 1940s until shortly before his death in 1991, Eugene Forsey directed over 800 letters to these editors, extolling his causes and pillorying opponents of his views.

When defending Canada, Forsey found himself deeply embroiled in the Québec nationalism controversy. It was an issue that swallowed up a lot of his time and energy during the last 30 years of his life and that even led to his resignation from the New Democratic Party because of its adoption of the two-nations doctrine.

In his passionate fight for a united Canada, Forsey denounced "dishonest" Québec nationalists who try to "pre-empt the adjective 'national' for Québec institutions" and wrote and spoke out strongly against the Meech Lake Accord, the series of controversial proposals designed to satisfy Québec's objections to the Canada Constitution Act of 1982. He reserved his harshest comments for the accord's 'distinct society' clause, dismissing it as "just the old open-ended 'special status' with a wig and whiskers."

When asked why he devoted so much time and thought to writing letters to newspaper editors, Forsey replied, "Perhaps letters to the editor may be a useful form of participatory democracy. Perhaps even one voice, shouting a good cause loud enough and long enough, may produce some effect, even on ideas, policies and governments which seem impregnable."

The author of these pungent and witty letters was born in Grand Bank, Newfoundland on May 29, 1904, to Eugene Forsey of that town and Florence Elvira Bowles of Ottawa. Descended from West Country of England stock, Eugene Forsey Sr. was noted for his eloquence and, in his youth, exceptional strength. He chalked up a brilliant academic record at secondary school in St. John's before enrolling at Mount Allison University in Sackville, New Brunswick, where he met Forsey's mother. Both graduated in 1899, Forsey's father in Arts and Theology and his mother in Arts.

After her husband's untimely death in 1904, when her son was just under six months of age, Elvira Forsey returned to her family in Ottawa, where Eugene Forsey was raised. In fact, when growing up in the home of his bilingual grandfather, the Chief Clerk of Votes and Proceedings of the House of Commons, young Forsey lived almost within the precincts of the House of Commons. As soon as he could walk, he trudged off to the interim Parliament Buildings in the Victoria Museum (now the Museum of Nature), where the House sat for three years after the 1916 fire. Later, he became a regular visitor to the House of Commons in the Centre Block.

Eugene Forsey lived with his grandparents and his mother at 311 Lisgar Street until 1922, obtaining all his schooling within a four-block radius of the family home. His brilliant academic career at Ottawa Collegiate Institute (now Lisgar Collegiate) was followed by four years at McGill University, where he enrolled in Honours Economics and Political Science, with half-Honours in English.

In his year of graduate study at McGill, Forsey wrote his MA thesis on economic and social aspects of the Nova Scotia coal industry. He capped his distinguished McGill record by winning a Rhodes scholarship to Oxford University in 1926.

Although he had been an Arthur Meighen Conservative during his McGill student days, Forsey returned from Oxford in 1929 a socialist and it was as a socialist that he lectured in economics and political science at McGill between 1929 and 1941. In 1933, while still in his twenties, he helped to draft the Regina Manifesto, which launched the Co-operative Commonwealth Federation (CCF), the forerunner of the National Democratic Party.

Eugene Forsey's activities in the CCF, the League for Social Reconstruction, the Fellowship for a Christian Social Order, the Montreal Civil Liberties Union and a visit to Russia in 1932 did not endear him to McGill's administration, which was undoubtedly under pressure from a Montreal elite badly scared by the Great Depression. He was therefore quick to accept a Guggenheim Fellowship that allowed him to quit teaching in 1941 and move to Cambridge, Massachusetts with his wife Harriet, whom he had married in 1935. There, with his newly minted McGill PhD, Forsey embarked on a book on the Canadian cabinet system.

Upon his return to Canada, in 1942, Eugene Forsey joined the Canadian Congress of Labour (later the Canadian Labour Congress) as Director of Research. He served in this capacity from 1942 to 1969, during which time he was the principal spokesman for organized labour in Canada and began work on *Trade Unions in Canada* 1812-1902, published in 1982.

While fighting labour movement battles in the 1940s, Eugene Forsey also made four unsuccessful bids for political office, initially as a candidate for Montreal's city council. Later, in Ottawa, he was a CCF candidate in a provincial election. In his first federal attempt he was pitted against George Drew, then seeking a seat as leader of the Conservatives.

During most of his stint at the labour congress Forsey also gave a course in Canadian government at Carleton University. He continued university teaching after his retirement from the congress, but at Queen's, Trent and then the University of Waterloo.

Eugene Forsey accepted an appointment to the Senate as a Liberal on October 7, 1970. True to form, however, he quit the Liberal ranks when the government introduced measures that he could not countenance.

"I simply wanted to resume my independence and I did so," he declared.

After retiring from the Senate in 1979, Eugene Forsey devoted his remaining years to writing and to fighting for a Canada that would be much more than "just a splash on the map." He died on February 20, 1991, survived by his two daughters, Helen and Margaret, and two grandchildren, his wife Harriet having predeceased him in 1988.

PHILANTHROPISTS

Throughout the world there are people who take seriously the obligation to employ their spare time and funds to support causes that they believe in. When their resources allow them to make substantial contributions to these causes they are often called philanthropists.

In nineteenth and early twentieth-century Ottawa, when there was no social security net or public welfare and hospitals were privately endowed, philanthropists, such as John Rudolphus Booth (profiled in the Entrepreneur section) and Alexander Smith Woodburn (profiled in the Entrepreneur section), played a vital role in advancing the interests of benevolent societies, hospitals, orphans' homes and homes for the aged etc. Unlike these male figures, however, the women profiled in this section were noted not so much for helping to fund these organizations and similar causes but for the time, energy and vision they contributed to them and, in Trudi Le Caine's case, for the zeal they brought to promoting the establishment of cultural organizations.

LADY ADELINE FOSTER
TEMPERANCE REFORMER, AUTHOR
AND VOLUNTEER PAR EXCELLENCE

(1844–1919)

When she died in 1919, Lady Foster, wife of prominent Conservative, Sir George Foster, was acclaimed as one of Ottawa's "estimable women" and her death described as a great loss to the women of the capital.

This fulsome praise was richly deserved according to the *Ottawa Citizen* since "few women in Canada [had] identified themselves so nobly with the organizations and institutions of the country as did Lady Foster."

Given Lady Foster's high profile, it is not surprising that her funeral, on September 19, 1919, was attended by a host of luminaries, including Their Excellencies the Duke and Duchess of Devonshire, Mackenzie King, who would succeed Robert Borden as prime minister, and Arthur Meighen, then a member of the Borden government.

It may come as a surprise, therefore, that few, if any, members of the Ottawa establishment were prepared to receive Adeline Foster when she arrived in the capital in 1889. Although personable, accomplished and newly married to a rising Conservative star, George Foster, she was definitely not welcome in official Ottawa—all because she had been a divorcée before her marriage to Foster.

Thanks to the interdiction of Lady Macdonald, who ruled official Ottawa with a rod of iron, Adeline Foster was not received at Earnscliffe (the Macdonald's home), Government House or just about anywhere else for that matter.

The ostracism only ended in late 1893, by which time the Fosters had returned to Ottawa after living in Toronto and Lord and Lady Aberdeen had been installed at Government House. To the redoubtable Lady Aberdeen, a fervent liberal, goes the credit for paving the way for Adeline Foster to be welcomed into Ottawa society.

In the eyes of the Aberdeens, it was grossly unfair that Mrs. Foster had never been received at Rideau Hall. "She divorced her husband—an American—in America for cruelty & desertion for six years & married Mr Foster some time after. There has never been anything against her but because the divorce laws of the two countries are different she was kept out," wrote Lady Aberdeen in her journal in November 1893. Continued the activist Governor General's wife, "There has been a good deal of feeling about it & we are v. sure we are right in deciding in her favour."

"Deciding in her favour" refers to the Aberdeens' decision to give their official blessing to the Fosters' entrée into Ottawa society. To signal their approval, the vice-regal couple invited the couple to a concert at Rideau Hall. Before this function, held on December 20, 1893, His Excellency had a private interview with Mr. Foster, then finance minister, while Lady Aberdeen spoke to Mrs. Foster.

"I think we need not have the slightest fear about the correctness of our decision even according to strict court rules. They are so thankful - & Sir John Thompson [the prime minister and one of the few members of official Ottawa who had accepted the Fosters] is delighted," noted the journal.

The subject of all this controversy, Adeline Foster (she became Lady Foster when her husband was knighted in 1912), was born April 14, 1844 in Hamilton, Upper Canada, the eldest daughter of Milton Davis, a stagecoach proprietor, and Hannah Cook.

At Genesee Wesleyan Seminary in Lime, New York, where she studied as a young woman, Addie Davis distinguished herself by her "diligence, aptitude, and general proficiency." Following her graduation, she taught an infants' class in a Hamilton Methodist Sunday school, where she met her first husband, D. B. Chisholm, then school superintendent and a prominent barrister. They married in 1864.

Regrettably, the marriage was not a happy one and in September 1883, according to Addie Chisholm, her husband deserted her and her young son and fled Hamilton, ostensibly because he had misappropriated clients' funds.

Sometime later, Addie Chisholm moved to Ottawa, where she earned money by renting out rooms in her Bank Street residence. One of her lodgers was George Foster, then a Conservative MP, and, like his future wife, a temperance advocate. A relationship developed between the two and in 1888, she moved from Ottawa to Chicago. It was there she obtained her divorce before marrying George Foster on July 2, 1889.

In the 1880s, before her divorce and remarriage, Addie Chisholm put her formidable organizational skills to work on behalf of the temperance movement, becoming second president of the Ontario Women's Christian

Temperance Union (1882-1888), Canadian representative to a National WCTU meeting in the United States in 1888, and publisher and editor of the WCTU periodical, the *Woman's Journal*. She also authored a number of pamphlets and tracts, including "*Why and How: A Handbook for Use of the W.C.T. Union in Canada.*"

Interestingly, this strong-willed but invariably tactful and kind leader advocated the female franchise in Ontario as an important step to obtaining legislated prohibition against alcohol.

After her marriage to George Foster, Addie Foster shifted gears. Instead of immersing herself in the temperance movement, she took up humanitarian and cultural pursuits.

In the capital, she became the first president of the Ottawa district board of management of the Victorian Order of Nurses and a member of the central board of management of the VON. A woman of many interests, she also became honorary president of the Local Council of Women, a member of the Morning Music Club of Ottawa's executive and a lifelong member of the Ottawa Humane Society and the Women's Historical Society, holding the office of president in the latter two organizations.

As president of the Women's Canadian Club of Ottawa and a member of the Ottawa and Ottawa Valley Branch of the Canadian Red Cross Society, this remarkable woman made a significant contribution to the First World War effort. According to the *Ottawa Citizen*, "It was she who led the Women's Canadian Club to the highest of its splendid war work, much of which was directly due to her wise guidance and fine patriotic spirit."

As part of her personal contribution, Lady Foster knitted warm woollen garments for Canadian soldiers at the front and exhorted Canadians to save food. "There is practically no restriction in the quantity or variety of consumption and no sacrifice in Canada comparable with that being made in England or France or Italy," she observed and then noted that radical changes in the Foster household had led to the serving of fish at least three days a week and the avoidance of all waste.

Lady Foster died on September 17, 1919, at the family residence on Somerset Street after what her biographer in the *Canadian Dictionary of Biography*, Sharon Anne Cook, describes as a two-year battle with breast cancer and what the local papers referred to as a "lingering illness of more than three months' duration."

Whatever the duration of the illness, there is no question but that the end came quickly and unexpectedly as Sir George had to be summoned back from Paris, where he was serving as a Canadian delegate to the 1919 Peace Conference. There is also no disputing the fact that the loss of this woman, who was once shunned by Ottawa society, was keenly felt. As Mrs. W. M. Southam expressed it, "Lady Foster's death removes one of the Capital's most charming and lovable women."

LILLIAN FREIMAN
OTTAWA'S JEWISH FLORENCE NIGHTINGALE

(1885–1940)

If there is one characteristic that stands out in the life of Lillian Freiman it is her selfless devotion to helping others less fortunate than herself. Indeed, her tireless efforts on behalf of needy individuals, Canada's war veterans and Zionism led *Canadian Heroes, The National Magazine for Young Canadians* to dub her "Mother to Thousands" and to declare, that "love of people was the essence of the life of Lillian Freiman..."

These sentiments were echoed by the *Ottawa Citizen*, which reported on Monday, November 4, 1940, "Ottawa lost one of its most beloved citizens, Canadian Jewry one of its most ardent workers and this country's war veterans a "mother" in the death Saturday of Mrs. A. J. Freiman, O.B.E."

The recipient of these richly deserved accolades was born in Mattawa, Ontario on June 6, 1885, to Lithuanian-born Moses Bilsky and his wife Pauline, daughter of an affluent Brooklyn businessman. Prior to settling in Mattawa, the adventurous Moses had moiled for gold in the Cariboo, fought on the Union side in the American Civil War, become a gun-runner in the Mexican Civil War, and lived and worked in Ottawa and Montreal.

When Lillian was only six, her strapping father decided to move once again: this time from Mattawa to Ottawa. In the nation's capital, the colourful Bilsky quickly made his influence felt, establishing a jewellery shop on Confederation Square and helping to found Ottawa's first synagogue on Murray Street.

From humble origins, Moses Bilsky became a prosperous businessman and a leading member of Ottawa's Jewish community. He was also a generous man who performed many acts of charity at a time when the city provided only ad hoc relief. Inspired by his example, young Lillian quickly embraced what would be a lifelong interest in helping the less fortunate. Emulating her father, she also became, at age 17, a committed Zionist.

As one of Moses' and Pauline's 11 children, Lillian grew up in a lively household that received a constant stream of both Jewish and non-Jewish visitors. Most of these were recent immigrants who were assisted not only by Moses but also by Pauline, who provided meals and washed and mended the clothing of newcomers.

When asked later in life if her parents' constant acts of charity had irked their children, Lillian, according to her son, Lawrence, replied,

"Good gracious no. It was as much the ordinary routine as going to school, eating, and going to sleep.

"We didn't know any other way of living. It was the usual thing when we came home from school to find that our rooms had been given to some unexpected visitor. We never knew where we were sleeping or how many of us would occupy a room. And we never knew when we went to dress what article of clothing would be missing."

When a new house furnishings store opened on Rideau Street, a curious Lillian went there to meet the two partners. After becoming acquainted with handsome, charming Archibald Jacob Freiman, she learned that they shared the same June 6 birthday, although the young merchant was five years older. Not long after, on August 18, 1903, when she was 18, they married.

Lillian continued to help the poor and needy following her marriage. In the family mansion at 149 Somerset St. West, the nerve centre of her operations, she met what her son Lawrence described as her "clients," men and women of all races and faiths and from around the world that came seeking help, sound advice and understanding. All of these, they unfailingly received from Lillian.

Long before women's liberation became a movement, Lillian Freiman fought for the establishment of a day nursery that would provide good child care for working mothers. With Mother Superior Mary Thomas Aquinas, she helped to found the Jeanne d'Arc Institute for "wayward girls," as pregnant, unmarried women, girls from reform institutions and girls who did not have jobs were called in those days. Indefatigable Lillian also worked for the setting up of a home training centre for domestic workers and the establishment of homes for elderly women that would allow them to live with greater dignity in their later years.

Despite having three children by the time the First World War erupted, Lillian still managed to make a major contribution to the war effort. She raised funds for European Jewry, opening an office for this purpose, organized weekly gatherings of Jewish women to sew and knit clothing for soldiers and helped soldiers' dependents adapt to their new life. For her work, she was affectionately called "Godmother" of the Ottawa branch of the Canadian Legion, of which she was an honorary member.

In an effort to aid veterans, Lillian Freiman, in the early 1920s, organized the women of Ottawa to make poppies. Later she became the only woman on the Dominion Poppy Committee. In fact, "Poppy Day" became closely identified with Mrs. Freiman, who made an invaluable contribution to the success of the annual campaign, the proceeds of which were used to assist unfortunate war veterans.

When the virulent flu epidemic of 1918 struck Ottawa, Mayor Harold Fisher asked Lillian Freiman to take full charge as the emergency administrator. For days on end she did not return home, snatching only a few hours' rest each day on a chesterfield in the mayor's office.

In 1920, Lillian Freiman spearheaded a campaign to bring hungry, homeless, Jewish orphans in the Ukraine to Canada. This involved her not only in fund raising but also in train-travel across Canada and a trip to the Ukraine, where she met the 150 fortunate children chosen by an advance delegation.

Although she worked tirelessly for many causes and appeals, including the Salvation Army and the Canadian National Institute for the Blind, Mrs. Freiman perhaps became best-known for her involvement with Canadian Hadassah, a volunteer women's Zionist organization that provides moral and material support to women, children and youth in Israel. From 1924 until her death in 1940, Lillian Freiman served continuously as Canadian Hadassah's president. Her inspired leadership prompted Zionism's founder, Dr. Theodore Herzl, to describe her as "one of the outstanding women in the world Zionist movement."

In 1934, in recognition of her volunteer work, Lillian Freiman was named an officer of the Order of the British Empire. She was the first Jewish person to be invested with the OBE. Two years later, in 1936, she was presented with the Vimy medal for her devoted work on behalf war veterans.

Not even a longstanding heart ailment that confined her to bed in 1939 prevented this indomitable woman from sending supplies to war-ravaged

Europe. When she eventually died, in Montreal's Royal Victoria Hospital, on November 2, 1940, Ottawa went into mourning. As the *Ottawa Citizen* noted, the capital had lost "one of its most beloved citizens, Canadian Jewry was now missing one of its most ardent workers and this country's war veterans were now without a 'mother.'"

LOTTA HITSCHMANOVA
FOUNDER, UNITARIAN SERVICE COMMITTEE OF CANADA

(1909–1990)

Attired in an army nurse's uniform and military-style hat, she travelled yearly to strife-torn and poverty-stricken parts of the world searching out towns and villages in need of Canadian assistance to recover from drought, war, disease and poverty.

At home, in Ottawa, she set off each September on a three-month trek across Canada to tell audiences about the hunger and destitution in other countries, to furnish particulars about how Canadian contributions in previous years had been employed and to renew her appeal for funds and clothing.

The petite, iron-willed woman who undertook these far-flung travels each year was Lotta Hitschmanova who founded the Unitarian Service Committee of Canada in 1945 and then directed it for 38 years, establishing 150 aid programs in 20 countries.

Lotta, as she was known, was Czech not Canadian by birth. She was born in Prague on November 28, 1909, to Max Hitschmann, who came from a poor Bohemian family, and Else Theiner, a socially ambitious and elegant woman fluent in several languages. Lotta would be joined by her only sibling, Lilly, fifteen months later.

By the time the sisters arrived their father had become a successful malt merchant with factories located beyond Prague's suburbs. The children were therefore raised in privileged surroundings with a cook, parlour maid and live-in nanny.

Both parents were determined that their daughters would be well-educated, with the result that Lotta graduated with honours from a coeducational high school, Stephans Gymnasium, and then, in 1929, enrolled in the faculty of Philosophy at the University of Prague. There, she immersed herself in the study of languages, but, after completing three terms, she persuaded her father to let her take the two middle years of her four-year course at the Sorbonne in Paris.

Over the next six years Lotta would scoop up diplomas in five languages from Prague University as well as a diploma in French studies, awarded by the Sorbonne through the Institute Français Ernest Denis in Prague. She would also manage to earn a scholarship that led to her completing a PhD from Prague University.

Enamoured of the intellectual life in Paris, young Lotta began studying political science and journalism at the Sorbonne in 1933. At this juncture in her life she entertained hopes of becoming a journalist and then eventually taking up a career in diplomacy. Accordingly, after obtaining a journalism diploma, in 1935, she returned to Czechoslovakia to pursue a career as a freelance journalist.

In turbulent, pre-war Europe, overworked Lotta poured her energies into writing for several newspapers as well as the Yugoslav government's news agency. Although she didn't belong to a political party, she pulled no punches in expressing anti-Nazi sentiments in her articles. This, not surprisingly, made her persona non grata to the Germans after Hitler seized a third of Czechoslovakia following the Munich Agreement of September 30, 1938.

Heeding the advice of Czech government officials, Lotta fled her homeland, joining a stream of fellow Czechs headed for Paris. There, she registered for a literature course at the University of Paris, but finding the capital's atmosphere too pro-Munich and too collaborative, she soon left the city for Brussels. It was about this time that she also began to employ the Slavic version of her surname—Hitschmanova rather than Hitschmann—to demonstrate her dislike of things German.

In Belgium, Lotta worked as a journalist, but when the Germans invaded that country she escaped to France, eventually ending up in Marseilles, where she was able to obtain employment with an immigration service that assisted refugees. One day, while queuing in Marseilles's market over lunch hour, she keeled over from fatigue and hunger.

After regaining consciousness, Lotta made her way to a medical clinic run by the Boston-based Unitarian Service Committee. This, claims her biographer, Clyde Sanger, would be her first contact with the organization. She would become even more familiar with it in January 1942 when she was appointed liaison officer with the Czechoslovak relief agency, Centre d'Aide Tsechoslovaque, but not until 1945 would the USC become her life's major work and mission.

In 1942, Lotta was able to escape from Europe by sailing from Lisbon to New York on a refugee-packed twin-screw steamer designed to carry bananas rather than passengers. After delivering a USC report to Boston, she quickly departed for Canada, which, unlike the United States, had granted her a visa.

Lotta later claimed she reached Montreal "exhausted, with a feeling of absolute solitude in an entirely strange country...I came with $60 in my pocket. I had an unpronounceable name. I weighed less than 100 lbs, and I was completely lost."

She was not lost for long for on her fourth day in this country she managed to obtain a secretarial job with a Montreal firm. Within three months she was in Ottawa working as a postal censor for the Department of War Services.

After the ending of hostilities, Lotta was offered several jobs, including one involving the rehabilitation of children in Czechoslovakia. When she learned, however, that the war had claimed the lives of her beloved parents, she decided to stay in Canada.

Lotta remained in Ottawa as she had already begun, in July 1945, to organize a Canadian branch of the USC to undertake relief and reconstruction work in war-ravaged Europe. In 1948, American insistence that every program be run by an American led her to reorganize this committee as a completely independent organization, USC Canada.

By 1949, Lotta Hitschmanova was logging 17,000 km on her annual cross-Canada tour, speaking 96 times in 36 locations and raising $50,000. And Canada was responding enthusiastically. In fact, from 1945 on, this tireless, single-minded worker for mankind persuaded generations of Canadians to aid destitute children in post-war Europe, Japan, Korea, Vietnam, independent Bangladesh and India.

Thanks to her own journalism background, Lotta knew what was needed to make a story and used this expertise to full advantage. Reporters and editors dubbed her "The Atomic Mosquito" because of her continuing success in getting good media coverage.

Throughout the years, Dr. Hitschmanova received countless awards, including the Gold Medal from the Red Cross of France (1950), the Medal of St. Paul from Greece (1952), Officer of the Order of Canada (1972) and Companion of the Order of Canada (1980).

Although this passionate, articulate woman spent the final years of her life suffering from Alzheimer's disease, she succumbed to cancer. She died September 1, 1990, unmarried, having devoted her life to the service of others.

TRUDI LE CAINE
SCHOOL TEACHER AND ARTS PATRON

(1911–1999)

■

" I 'm glad I had a contribution to make and above all, I had a debt to pay to Canada," declared long-time Ottawa resident, tireless arts patron and member of the Order of Canada, Trudi Le Caine, when interviewed some years ago.

Just how large this cultural trailblazer's contribution was is made abundantly clear by a list of the numerous arts organizations in Ottawa that she helped to launch or promoted or both. The list includes not only the Eugene Kash Children's Concerts and the National Youth Orchestra but also the National Arts Centre, the National Arts Centre Orchestra Association, Opera Lyra, Le Groupe de la Place Royale (Ottawa's resident modern dance atelier) and Espace Musique (a contemporary music outlet).

Known aptly as Ottawa's "Mother of the Arts," and once described as a one-woman Canada Council, Trudi Le Caine was born Gertrude Janowski in 1911 in Passeau, Germany, near the border of Austria. She was raised in Czechoslovakia and was living in Berlin with her mother and stepfather, Arnold Walter, in 1933 when Adolf Hitler became chancellor of Germany and set out to establish an absolute dictatorship.

Shortly after Hitler's election, the indomitable young woman was beaten up one night while working for the liberal opposition. On learning that there was a warrant out for her arrest, she immediately escaped to Spain, soon to be engulfed in civil war. Leaving Spain, Le Caine fled to Paris, where she studied at the Sorbonne, qualifying as a teacher before France was invaded by the Germans in 1940.

In the wake of the German occupation, Trudi Le Caine headed for Canada, where her mother and stepfather had immigrated in 1937. She spent two years in Toronto, the Walters' new home, then accepted a position with the federal civil service, which necessitated a move to Ottawa. As a censor she was charged with censoring letters written by German prisoners-of-war in Canadian internment camps. By her own admission, it was not a job in which she excelled since she could never determine what constituted sensitive information. "All I did was correct the spelling and grammar," reported Le Caine years later.

Much more to her liking was her job as a French teacher for the Ottawa Board of Education. One of the several schools at which she taught was Mutchmore Public School, where she formed lasting friendships with many of her students.

At Broadview Public School she made such a forceful impression on one student that decades later the admiring woman could recount in detail an incident that illustrated her French teacher's sense of humour. Evidently on April 1, 1956, Trudi Le Caine strode into the classroom and handed out sheets of lined paper, announcing, as she made her way around the room, that she was springing a snap test. The surprised students glumly wrote their names on the sheets, as instructed, and then waited apprehensively. Le Caine allowed the tension to build and then declared, "April Fool," at which point everybody broke into gales of laughter.

It was in the mid-forties that Trudi Le Caine first became involved with local art organizations as a volunteer. Her inspiration was Lyla Rasminsky, wife of Bank of Canada governor Louis Rasminsky. "Lyla was my inspiration and she infected me with the bug of helping artists and artistic organizations about whom I felt strongly," recalled Le Caine during an interview.

No doubt another inspiration was her distinguished and beloved stepfather, Arnold Walter. A man of great energy, drive and creativity, he became director of the University of Toronto's faculty of music in 1952 and a highly respected music figure throughout the world. As a tireless promoter of musical projects, he was bound to have had a powerful influence on his stepdaughter.

When Lyla Rasminsky invited Trudi Janowski to become a patron of the Children's Concerts, the young woman could not refuse. Thus began her association with a much-needed series of low-cost concerts organized by a group of progressive women with the cooperation of Eugene Kash, then concert master of the Ottawa Philharmonic and music director of the National Film Board.

From then on there was no stopping the indomitable Trudi Janowski, who rolled up her sleeves and went to work, using her charm, legendary powers of persuasion and iron determination to help create a thriving arts scene in Ottawa. Certainly there was plenty of scope for her efforts. In fact, when this cultured European first arrived in the capital the list of cultural events for the entire year took up less than half a page in the September arts edition of the *Ottawa Citizen*.

In addition to becoming involved with children and music, serving as midwife to Opera Lyra, and helping to get Ottawans to rally around a national performing centre for the arts, this woman of seemingly inexhaustible energy assisted individual artists. To struggling young visual artists, she was a godsend, exhibiting examples of their work in her home and staging European-style salons to which she invited prospective patrons.

In addition to fighting for the arts, Trudi Le Caine waged a battle to introduce skating to the Rideau Canal. When she could not sell the idea to the mayor of the day, she approached the late Douglas Fullerton, then head of the National Capital Commission. Fullerton became an enthusiastic convert to Trudi's vision and in 1971, the canal was opened to skating, attracting some 18,000 skaters its first day of operation.

In 1960, when she was 48, Trudi Janowski married bachelor Hugh Le Caine, an eminent National Research Council scientist and pioneer of electronic music. Although the marriage brought her great happiness, it required considerable adjustment on her part. Part of this adjustment revolved around meal times. Since her husband's most productive hours of work were between 5:00 and 11:00 p.m., Trudi Le Caine, according to her husband's biographer, made a practice of always serving dinner at midnight

When her beloved husband suffered serious head injuries in a motorcycle accident in July 1976 Trudi Le Caine was devastated. Hugh Le Caine remained in a coma for almost two months, during which time his wife visited him in hospital every day. He eventually made a partial recovery, but then died almost a year later of a fatal stroke.

When Trudi Le Caine died in her Ottawa home on September 5, 1999, she did so secure in the knowledge that she had played a major role in the dramatic changes that had occurred in Ottawa's cultural landscape since her arrival in the capital over half-a-century ago and that she had, indeed, paid her debt to Canada.

PHYSICIANS

The first doctors who arrived in what is now Ottawa were employed by the British military to attend to the needs of workers hired to build the Rideau Canal, Canada's first mega construction project. In 1826, during initial planning for the canal's construction, arrangements were made for a subaltern's command of sixty soldiers to be stationed near each work site and for surgeons to be engaged and furnished with the necessary medicines. These men would have their work cut out for them, tending to injuries and treating the countless victims of typhoid, dysentery and swamp fever. Prominent among them was Edward Van Cortland, who subsequently served the civilian population and lived in Bytown until his death.

Among the first civilian doctors to practise in Bytown was colourful, but incompetent, Alexander J. Christie, who also became the settlement's first newspaper publisher. He hung up his shingle in 1827. Most of the medical care in Bytown was provided, however, by four nuns of the Sisters of Charity, headed by Mère Elisabeth Bruyère. No sooner had they arrived in Bytown from Montreal (February 20, 1845) than they began visiting and tending to the sick at home. That May they opened a humble hospital on St. Patrick Street. Dr. Van Cortland immediately offered his services, inspiring other doctors to follow his example. These included Drs. Robichaud, Lacroix, Land, Beaubien and Hill. Dr. Hamnett Hill, who immigrated to Canada in 1837, is one of the two physicians profiled in this section. The other doctor is Frederick Montizambert, a public health pioneer. He settled in the capital in 1899, a year after Dr. Hill's death.

DR. HAMNETT HILL

RESPECTED MEDICAL PRACTITIONER AND MASON

(1811–1898)

———■———

O ne of Ottawa's earliest and most respected medical practitioners was Dr. Hamnett Hill, a devout Mason and Tory whose descendents have played a leading role in the Ottawa community.

Born in London, England, in December 1811, the son of John Wilkes Hill, a surgeon, Hamnett Hill pursued his medical studies at the London Hospital. In 1834, he became a member of the Royal College of Surgeons and after practising in Brighton for three years he set sail for Canada.

The young doctor first settled in March Township, where he started a small practice and became acquainted with the cultured and wealthy Englishman, Hamnett Kirkes Pinhey, one of the founders of the famous March colony. In his earlier life Pinhey had been a prosperous London merchant who had graduated to produce-broker, trading on the continent with his own ships. He had given all this up to immigrate in 1820 to Upper Canada, planning to establish a model English estate in the wilderness of March township. Seeking to combine leisure with dignity, Pinhey embarked on an intensive building program that resulted in the construction of a large stone manor house, Horaceville, and several other buildings.

One of these stone edifices was St. Mary's Church, where, on May 18, 1844, Hamnett Hill married Pinhey's daughter, Mary Ann. The following year, Mary Ann gave birth to a son, Hamnett Pinhey, who would become, like his father, a well-known doctor. Sadly, the next decade saw three Hill children die at a very young age.

By the time he married Mary Ann Pinhey, Hamnett Hill had traded life in March for life in Bytown. When he settled there, in 1842, Bytown was a backwoods village of just over 3,000 people, most of whom were Irish or French and Roman Catholic. A lusty, brawling settlement, it lacked sidewalks and paved streets and was heavily dependent on the lumber industry.

Canada's future capital would be Hamnett Hill's home for the next 56 years, during which time the up-and-coming doctor would establish an extensive and lucrative medical practice and become "much esteemed" as a consultant. While doing so, he would also make his mark in the community at large.

The young doctor early demonstrated that he was a man of principle who would not be intimidated by the reputation of well-known colleagues. One such colleague was Dr. Edward Van Cortland, a physician noted for his remarkable skills, but also for his erratic behaviour and somewhat cavalier treatment of patients. In 1846, Dr. Hill accused Dr. Cortland of two of the grossest breaches of professional discourtesy: refusing to attend to a patient for him in his absence except under the express understanding that Dr. Hill would no longer be that patient's regular medical practitioner; and using "unprofessional language" at the beside of that patient.

After the accusations had been aired at a hearing, Dr. W. C. Seaman concluded that Dr. Hill had proved the first charge but not the second. When asked why he had allowed professional squabbles to become a "matter of public notoriety," Hamnett Hill replied that he wanted to "expose such conduct as that above to the severe scrutiny of public opinion." Such scrutiny, he hoped, would occasionally "restrain persons from the commission of 'dirty actions' which are not exactly amenable to any other code."

Hill next achieved prominence in the typhus epidemic of 1847. During the six weeks that it swept the community, from the middle of June to the end of August 1847, the epidemic claimed the lives of 314 people, most of them destitute Irish immigrants who had crossed the Atlantic in the malodorous holds of timber ships after fleeing the potato famine in their homeland.

When the epidemic broke out, Bytown boasted only an ad hoc health board, which, regrettably, had no health facilities at its disposal. Only one small hospital existed, the General Hospital, operated by the Catholic Sisters of Charity. With the arrival of the scourge, the Sisters immediately offered property that they had recently acquired to the Emigration Agent, George Burke, and, with the help of Father Telmon, a typhus hospital was erected on the site. Since many of the 3,000 immigrants who arrived in Bytown that summer were stricken with typhus, it wasn't long before more emigration sheds had to be thrown up and an addition built to the hospital.

Notable among the small corps of doctors, who volunteered to treat the sick, was Hamnett Hill. He was put in charge of the rude emigrant sheds that were converted into a hospital. And, not surprisingly, he too came down with typhus fever. In fact, in the *Packet* of August 28, 1847, there is a reference to the serious and almost hopeless condition of Dr. Hill. Fortunately he survived.

As a result of the epidemic, Protestants in Bytown agitated for the building of a Protestant hospital. Their efforts bore fruit when the cornerstone of the County of Carleton General Protestant Hospital, funded by a government grant and private subscriptions, was laid in 1850 and opened the following year. Dr. Hill was one of the incorporators and later a member of the hospital's staff. Still later he became consulting surgeon and, on the organization of the medical board, its chairman.

When a depression in 1849 triggered the Stony Monday Riots, Hamnett Hill again came to public attention. The immediate cause of the riots was a public meeting called to draft an invitation to the new governor general, Lord Elgin, to visit Bytown. Reformers and moderate Tories promoted such a visit, hoping that it would persuade the governor general to recommend Bytown as a suitable site for a new capital for the Canadas. Rabid Tories, however, vehemently opposed the idea of such a visit. Under no circumstances would they tolerate a governor general who had presided over the granting of "responsible" government.

Both factions attended the public meeting that convened Monday, September 17 and that shortly degenerated into a full-scale riot. While troops strove to quell the violence, the Tories reopened the meeting under Hamnett Hill's chairmanship and passed a motion censuring Lord Elgin's conduct.

Given his Tory stripes, it is not surprising that Hamnett Hill became a member of the Board of Commissioners of Police, formed in 1863. The board consisted of the Mayor, the Recorder and the Police Magistrate, Hamnett Hill.

Always a loyal member of his profession, Hamnett Hill also helped to found St. Luke's General Hospital (1898), which was located on Elgin Street. It became one of three institutions that merged to form the Ottawa Civic Hospital.

After he died on February 10, 1898, the *Ottawa Citizen* described Hamnett Hill as one of Ottawa's oldest and most respected residents and probably the oldest Mason in the city, having been for over 47 years a member of Dalhousie Lodge. Three years later, in 1901, a fellow physician, Dr. Beaumont Small, lauded the doctor for being "one in whom we can find our ideal."

DR. FREDERICK MONTIZAMBERT
PIONEER IN CANADIAN PUBLIC HEALTH

(1843–1929)

———■———

D escribed by the *Montreal Witness* as "a most able and industrious public servant", Dr. Frederick Montizambert was an internationally acclaimed public health pioneer, who made his home in Ottawa for almost 30 years.

A native of Québec City, Frederick Montizambert was born on February 3, 1843 to Edward Louis Montizambert, a law clerk in the Senate of Canada, and Lucy Irwin, daughter of Chief Justice Bowen of Québec. On his father's side, he was descended from the Bouchers, an old French family that had immigrated to New France in 1635. Among its distinguished members was the first governor of Trois-Rivères, Pierre Boucher; one of his sons took the name Boucher de Montizambert (after the family estate in France), thereby inaugurating the use of Montizambert as a family name in New France.

Young Frederick attended schools in St. Johns, Québec (now known as St-Jean-sur-Richelieu, Québec) and Toronto before going on to study medicine at Laval. He moved on to Edinburgh University where he was awarded prizes in chemistry, midwifery and surgery. In 1864, he obtained an M.D. degree and a licentiate in midwifery from the university. That same year he also acquired a licentiate in midwifery from the Royal College of Surgeons of Edinburgh, having "made the most creditable appearance of all who were examined at the same period."

Armed with his prestigious credentials, Montizambert returned to his hometown and entered into private medical practice. His stint in private practice was short-lived, however, because in 1865 he successfully petitioned for the position of visiting physician to the Marine and Emigrant Hospital in Québec. That same year, he also married Mary Jane, daughter of the late Honourable William Walker, member of Québec's legislative council.

In a glowing testimonial that accompanied Montizambert's petition for the hospital post, a fellow of the Royal College of Surgeons of Edinburgh lauded the young doctor for the "assiduity" and "great energy," with which he had applied himself to his studies. The fellow concluded, "The ability and industry which distinguished him as a student, will, I feel sure, continue to characterize him in after life, and will be exerted in the cause of humanity in such a manner as will greatly benefit any patients who are entrusted to his care..."

After serving as visiting physician to the Marine and Emigrant Hospital for a year, Frederick Montizambert entered the public health service of Canada, joining the medical staff of the Grosse-Île quarantine station. Three years later, in 1869, he was promoted to the post of medical superintendent of the station, established in 1832 as the principal port of arrival for immigrants to Canada. He would occupy this position for the next 30 years.

Grosse-Île quarantine station was located 48 kilometres downstream from Québec City. It had been set up during a period when approximately 30,000 British newcomers, the majority of them Irish, arrived each year at Québec, then the gateway to the Province of Canada. During this time, major epidemics of cholera and typhus raged on the Continent and in Great Britain. When colonial authorities learned that immigrants who had contracted cholera were about to arrive in Canada via the St. Lawrence, they promptly set up the Grosse-Île quarantine station.

Two years after it opened, the station battled another cholera outbreak. And in 1847-48, when some 100,000 immmigrants, many of them destitute Irish fleeing the potato famine, sailed for Québec, the station faced a still more deadly typhus epidemic. Not until 1854, after a recurrence of cholera, would Grosse-Île cease to handle virulent disease outbreaks.

When the hastily established station began operating, its facilities were ill-equipped to accommodate and properly treat huge numbers of people. To make matters worse, medical authorities were woefully lacking in knowledge about the causes, spread and treatment of infectious diseases. As a result, thousands of Irish immigrants died at Grosse-Île in 1847.

Memories of the "floating coffins"—as the overcrowded, unsanitary immigrant vessels were called—and the horrendous conditions that prevailed on Grosse-Île during these years were fresh in Dr. Montizambert's mind when he arrived on the island in 1866.

By the time the doctor became medical superintendent of Grosse-Île, however, Canada had taken over control of immigration from colonial authorities, and had drawn up a comprehensive policy on immigration and settlement. The way was thus paved for the creation of a more reliable, efficient quarantine station.

Frederick Montizambert, who was knowledgeable about the newly discovered "microbes" and their relationship to contagion, was ideally suited to making this happen. Determined to stop the spread of disease, the hard-working superintendent laid out the island's facilities in such a way as to ensure that sick immigrants would not come into contact with healthy travellers or those under observation. In addition, he had vessels and luggage inspected and disinfected, and arranged for passengers to be examined and vaccinated.

As the years went by and immigration trends changed, Dr. Montizambert used available funds to renew the station's facilities, which included hospitals, accommodation for travellers, workers' houses and chapels, etc. According to historian André Sevigny, he also implemented stringent new quarantine regulations that eliminated laxity and loopholes.

During the navigation season Dr. Montizambert and his family lived on Grosse-Île. The rest of the year they took up residence in Toronto, which is where he learned, in 1894, that he had been appointed General Superintendent of the St. Lawrence Service.

A further career advancement occurred in 1899 when Frederick Montizambert was relieved of his duties at Grosse-Île and appointed Canada's first director general of public health. The new position carried with it the rank and precedence of deputy minister, although he retained the annual salary he was then receiving: $4,000.

With this appointment, Montizambert moved to Ottawa where he became very active in the community, serving for some years as rector's warden of Christ Church Cathedral, president of the Rideau Club, a dedicated worker for the Red Cross Society and the St. John Ambulance Association and director of the Perley Home for Incurables.

In his job as director general of public health, Dr. Montizambert supervised the federal government's dispersed health services, which included quarantine stations and two leper treatment facilities, the most notable being the one at Tracadie, New Brunswick. He also studied the use of Chaulmoogra oil in the treatment of leprosy.

During his long and distinguished career, Frederick Montizambert authored numerous papers and accumulated memberships in an eye-popping number of medical societies in Canada and the United States. In the final stages of his career, he was instrumental in helping to establish the federal department of health, but no sooner had the department come into being in 1919, than he resigned from the federal public service.

Dr. Montizambert died in his Cooper Street home on November 2, 1929 after a long illness and was buried in Beechwood Cemetery. Reflecting on his passing, one paper noted that to the "lustre" of a brilliant medical career, Frederick Montizambert had "added the polish of an old world French culture."

The public health pioneer was survived by four daughters and one son, his wife having predeceased him in November of 1921.

PUBLIC SERVANTS

In October, 1865, before the new parliament buildings were completely finished, the first civil servants began arriving in Ottawa from Québec City, then the capital of the Province of Canada. Their numbers increased substantially when the federal government's expenditure on national services multiplied seven times between 1896 and 1913, in response to an economic boom and a dramatic increase in immigration. Their ranks increased more than two-fold in the following decade and dramatically during the Second World War, when Ottawa-based federal employees would come to dominate the Ottawa scene.

The men and women in the civil service come to Ottawa from all parts of the country and from a variety of political, ethnic, religious and cultural backgrounds. Canadians with a national outlook, they are a breed apart. Among them have been many outstanding and talented individuals, people such as J.R. Bourinot, Eric Brown and Marius Barbeau, who are profiled in this book.

SIR JOHN GEORGE BOURINOT

CANADA'S FIRST POLITICAL SCIENTIST

(1836–1902)

———————■———————

Anybody who has used *Bourinot's Rules of Order* when chairing a public meeting owes a debt of gratitude to the well-known Ottawan and Victorian Canadian Sir John George Bourinot.

Today, he is best remembered as the original author of this procedural manual. Sir John, however, was much more than just an expert on parliamentary procedure. At various times in his multi-faceted life he was also recognized as a journalist, parliamentary reporter, historian, littérateur and expert in constitutional law, who was consulted by governors general, prime ministers, lieutenant governors and provincial premiers on constitutional matters.

John George Bourinot was born in Sydney, Nova Scotia on October 24, 1836, the first child of John and Margaret Jane Bourinot. His father, who was of Huguenot descent, was one of Sydney's most prominent citizens, serving at different times as a justice of the peace, a lieutenant-colonel in the Cape Breton reserve militia, French consul in Sydney, a member of Nova Scotia's House of Assembly, and a member of the Canadian Senate. His mother came from the "blue blood" Marshall family, which had United Empire Loyalist origins.

Perhaps because educational standards in Cape Breton at the time were so dismal, John George (to distinguish him from his father) was educated at home by a private tutor, the Rev. William Young Porter. Porter was amazed at his pupil's precociousness and took great pains to encourage his progress. Partly because of his tutor's diligence, young Bourinot was admitted to Trinity College in Toronto in 1854. Despite his passion for study and his academic success, however, he left Trinity in 1856 before obtaining a B.A. degree.

His departure from Trinity was followed by a brief stint at a Toronto paper, the *Leader*, where he reported on debates in the 1858 session of the parliament of the Province of Canada. With the close of the parliamentary session, Bourinot left Toronto to return to Sydney, but not before marrying Bridget Delia Houck, an illiterate widow who bore him two sons.

In Sydney, Bourinot dabbled briefly in law, serving as an articled clerk to attorney James McKeagney. After relinquishing his clerkship, he moved to Québec and then possibly to the United States. In July of 1860, he returned to Nova Scotia, where he made Halifax his home. There, he became first a newspaper proprietor and editor, and shortly afterwards, a reporter to the Nova Scotia House of Assembly.

Fifteen months after arriving in the provincial capital, Bourinot lost his wife; she died shortly after giving birth to their second child, a son. He remained a widower until 1865 when he married Emily Alden Pilsbury, the daughter of the Honourable Albert Pilsbury and his wife, Abigail Cunningham Porter.

Bourinot left the *Halifax Evening Reporter* and gave up his job as reporter to the House of Assembly after spending seven years in Halifax. He went back to Sydney, this time to earn a living as a freelance writer. His choice of topics ranged from the geography, history and future of his native province, especially that of Cape Breton, to statesmanship and letters. Bourinot also tried his hand at fiction, some of which provided a sympathetic treatment of the Indians.

John George Bourinot moved to the Ottawa area in the spring of 1869 when he was appointed to "the vacant English clerkship" in the Canadian Senate. Initially the Bourinot family lived in Hull. However, his biographer, Margaret Banks claims that sometime before March of 1872, he moved to Ottawa, which became Bourinot's home until his death in 1902.

Bourinot's first impressions of the national capital were not flattering. In a letter published in 1870, he complained that the city was dull, especially during the winter months when the only available entertainment was "Penny Readings." The logical location for Canada's capital, he opined, was Montreal, "the natural metropolis of the Dominion."

His opinion of Ottawa soon changed. By 1873 he was lauding it as a lively place where cabinet ministers hosted dinner parties and evening events, and their wives entertained at receptions and reunions. Some of this transformation, he declared, could be attributed to Rideau Hall, which was no longer the staid place that it had once been. Now it boasted a vice-regal couple noted for their hospitality and a new ballroom in which "theatrical parties" were staged.

In the spring of 1873, Bourinot was appointed second clerk assistant in the House of Commons. He served as assistant clerk until late 1880, when he was appointed to the coveted position of clerk. When describing his new duties, he reported that the Chief Clerk, who sits at the head of the table... is sworn to make "true entries, remembrances, and journals of the things done and passed in the House of Commons."

In the 22 years that he served as clerk, John George Bourinot became an eminent authority on parliamentary procedure and constitutional law. It was as an expert on parliamentary procedure that he wrote *Bourinot's Rules of Order* in 1884. Reflecting on the differences between the British and Canadian political systems, he observed, "In the course of years divergences of practice have arisen, and a great many precedents have been made which seem to call for a work such as this."

During his years in Ottawa, Bourinot wrote extensively not only on parliamentary procedure but also on constitutional law and history. Among his noted works were two general histories of Canada and the *Manual of the Constitutional History of Canada*.

He also produced one published novel, *Marguerite*, and, in 1881, he broached the innovative idea of a national library for Canada. That same year he became a charter member of the Royal Society of Canada, which elected him president in 1892.

The recipient of many honours during his lifetime, John George Bourinot died in his Cooper Street home on October 13, 1902. He left his wife, Isabelle Cameron (whom he had married after the death of his second wife, Emily,) three sons and a daughter, and a reputation as Canada's first political scientist.

ARTHUR PERCY SHERWOOD

A LIFE OF PUBLIC SERVICE

(1854–1940)

W hen he entered this world on March 18, 1854, Arthur Percy Sherwood became an instant member of one of Ottawa's most distinguished families, a decided advantage when it came to carving out an outstanding career in the Ottawa police force, and subsequently the Dominion Police.

A son of Edward Sherwood, registrar of Carleton County, and a grandson of Judge Livius Peters Sherwood of Brockville, Percy, as he was known, graduated from the Ottawa Grammar School in 1875. After graduation he worked for the Imperial Bank of Canada, but deciding that a banker's life was not for him, he left after two years to become deputy sheriff of Carleton County.

This was a wise move since it made good use of the young man's genius for organization and his capacity for human understanding and kindliness. These would serve him well as a deputy sheriff and then as chief of Ottawa's small police force (1879-1882). In this latter capacity he did much to modernize the force's various departments, and thereby improve its overall efficiency.

An even greater challenge awaited Percy Sherwood when, in 1882, he left the Ottawa police force to reorganize the Dominion Police. So successfully did he undertake this task that in 1885 he was promoted from Superintendent to Commissioner. That same year, in the first of his many official out-of-town assignments, he personally delivered the order for Louis Riel's execution to the Lieutenant-Governor of the Northwest Territories, Edgar Dewdney.

Established by the federal government in 1868, following the assassination of Thomas D'Arcy McGee, the Dominion Police's chief function was to guard the Parliament Buildings in Ottawa. It also furnished bodyguards for prominent government figures and operated an intelligence service, whose agents infiltrated the Irish-American branch of the militant Fenian brotherhood.

During Percy Sherwood's service in the Dominion Police (he retired from it in 1919, one year before it was absorbed by the RCMP) the force increased in size and importance. Notable among the new responsibilities that it adopted was the operation of a Canadian fingerprinting bureau. It traced its establishment to an initiative taken by Edward Foster, a Dominion Police constable, who heard about the new science of fingerprinting while attending a meeting of the International Association of Police Chiefs in 1904 in St. Louis, then hosting the World Fair. Foster was so inspired by what he learned that he wrote to Percy Sherwood requesting permission to stay on in St. Louis to further study fingerprinting. Permission was granted.

Two years later the Commissioner demonstrated once again that he was first and foremost a practical, but visionary, police officer when he headed a chief constables' deputation that urged Canada's Minister of Justice to adopt a proposal for a centralized fingerprint bureau to be maintained at government expense under the jurisdiction of the Dominion Police. The minister approved the proposal, but the new National Fingerprint Bureau was not created until 1910, and then only after a notorious criminal had escaped from the Kingston Penitentiary.

Percy Sherwood was one of the moving spirits behind the establishment of the Chief Constables' Association of Canada, serving at one time as its president. He was also a charter member of the International Association of Chiefs of Police of the United States and Canada. When the organizations met in annual convention, he made valuable presentations on all aspects of police work. Indeed, Percy Sherwood became so well-known and highly regarded as an expert on police matters that police chiefs across the country consulted him.

While serving as Commissioner of the Dominion Police, Percy Sherwood became involved with the Bering Sea question. Instigated by the actions of the Americans, who in 1886 began seizing Canadian sealing vessels in the disputed Bering Sea, the controversy generated heated indignation across Canada. The dispute was finally settled by an arbitration tribunal in 1893, but not before a small squadron of the Royal Navy had ominously taken up its station at Esquimalt, near Victoria.

The federal government, determined to procure certain evidence for the arbitration proceedings, selected Percy Sherwood for the job. This he discharged personally, obtaining affidavits from seamen in British Columbia and San Francisco. The information that he acquired proved so valuable he was officially thanked by a special order-in-council.

As Dominion Police Commissioner, Percy Sherwood was in charge of police and detective arrangements for the royal visit made by their Royal Highnesses, the Duke and Duchess of Cornwall and York (later

King George V and Queen Mary), to Canada in 1901. For this he was specially commended in a letter from His Royal Highness to the Governor General. Sir Percy, who was knighted in 1916, also served as honorary aide-de-camp to all governors general from the Earl of Minto to Lord Byng.

Outside of his police work, Sir Percy took a keen interest in the Boy Scouts of Canada, serving as chief commissioner of the organization from its establishment until 1918. Thanks to his expertise in rifle shooting and his organizing ability, he became president of the Dominion of Canada Rifle Association, and in 1903 he commanded the Canadian Bisley team.

Sir Percy maintained a long association with the 43rd Regiment, Duke of Cornwall's Own Rifles, which he commanded from 1898 to 1904. He commanded the 8th Infantry Brigade from 1908 to 1911 and on November 6, 1930, he was appointed Honorary Colonel of the Cameron Highlanders of Ottawa, a post he held until his death.

One of those rare individuals who cultivates friends from all walks of life, Percy Sherwood joined Edward Bremner and R. Gordon Edwards in founding a men's group, the Laurentian Club, in 1904. At a time when Ottawa society was highly stratified and membership in men's associations was restricted to individuals who were well-connected, he sought a club where he could mingle with all of his many friends, no matter what their origins or occupation.

At his death on October 15, 1940, Sir Percy was survived by his wife, the former Esther Alberta Slater, and his two sons and four daughters.

In its tribute to him, the *Ottawa Journal* wrote, "If the real test of the fineness of a man's character can be gauged by the number of friends who sincerely mourn his passing, Sir Percy Sherwood was one of the finest. Throughout his long and highly honourable life he made friends everywhere. He was, in fact, one of those fortunate individuals who look out rather than in, whose mind was not so much concerned with his own interests that he could find no time to delight in other people's happiness or to sympathize with their sorrows."

WILLIAM TERRILL MACOUN
CANADA'S FIRST DOMINION HORTICULTURALIST

(1869–1933)

Today, a captivating sunken garden, one of several different areas that make up the Central Experimental Farm's Ornamental Gardens, commemorates his name.

Yet of the thousands of visitors who stroll through this favourite wedding party location each summer, probably only a handful realize that it takes its name from Canada's first Dominion Horticulturalist and that his official residence, a large imposing shingled house, once occupied this site.

The Macoun Memorial Garden opened in 1936, the fiftieth anniversary of the Farm's establishment, and only three years after William Terrill Macoun died. Wishing to commemorate his work and impressive legacy, the federal government had had his house torn down and the site transformed into a garden designed by Warren Oliver, employed by the then Horticultural Division of the Research Branch.

Thanks to Oliver's plan, which incorporated features of Macoun's original garden, today's visitors to the memorial garden can view not only a recessed pond and low stone embankments crowned with flowers, but also a perennial border that Macoun had planted and many of the trees and shrubs that had surrounded his Farm home.

The man who inspired this garden was born in Belleville, Ontario on January 17, 1869 to John Macoun and his wife Ellen, née Terrill, of Brighton, Ontario.

A native of Northern Ireland, John Macoun had immigrated in his late teens to Canada West in 1850, settling with his family on a farm in Seymour Township. Never enamoured of farming, he would go on to become a graduate of Syracuse University (MA), teacher, self-taught botanist, noted civil servant, author and this country's foremost field naturalist. He would also become a tireless champion of the agricultural potential of Canada's Western interior.

Given his father's passions, it is not surprising that young William Macoun took the career direction he did. In fact, his early interest in botany took root in 1882 when John Macoun moved his family to Ottawa, having been named Dominion Botanist to the Geological Survey of Canada the previous year.

Young William Macoun attended Albert College in Belleville, Ontario and Ottawa's Lisgar Collegiate Institute. In 1888, he joined the staff of the recently established Central Experimental Farm as Horticultural Assistant to the Director, William Saunders.

In no time at all, the new recruit was drawing attention to his capacity for hard work. Writing to her husband, William Saunders, in 1890, when he was away on one of his many business trips, Agnes Saunders reported, "I see a light in your office at nights. Will Macoun works there almost every night."

The botanist's dedication and ability resulted in his being appointed Horticulturalist and Curator of the Arboretum and Botanical Garden in 1895. He was named Chief of the Horticultural Division in 1898.

Since he has been described in a Friends of the Farm brief as a "man who wrote much, spoke much, and did much," it was inevitable that William Macoun would greatly influence the work of the Horticultural Division. Fortunately, he was able to bring a personal knowledge of growing conditions throughout Canada to this work as he and his brother, James Melville, had travelled with their father on field trips in Western Canada and Québec.

One of William Macoun's more notable achievements involved the establishment of arboreta of both native and newly introduced species of shrubs and trees at each of Canada's experimental farms. This was done with a view to developing an extensive list of material suitable for planting on farm homesteads across the country. Largely through his efforts, Ottawa's Arboretum boasted over 3,000 species of shrubs and trees by 1900.

Macoun's primary interest, however, was in apple-breeding. He made exhaustive studies of the blossoming periods of 68 varieties of apples, using information that had been supplied with the help of 48 observers from British Columbia's Salt Spring Island to Prince Edward Island. Using this data, the horticulturalist divided the different varieties into groups that he labelled "early," "medium" or "late-blooming." T.H. Astey reported in *One Hundred Harvests* that this practice enabled apple growers to plant the different varieties within a group close to one another, so that pollination could be optimized.

Macoun's apple-breeding program, which sought to combine winter hardiness with other horticultural traits, resulted in the introduction of 174 varieties, two of which, Lobo and Melba, are still popular.

It was the McIntosh apple, however, that held a special place in Macoun's heart. In his view, it required "no words of praise. It is one of the finest appearing and best dessert apples grown." Convinced by his research that it was ideally suited for the Canadian climate and the fast-developing urban market, he became one of its most enthusiastic promoters.

William Macoun's passion for horticulture led to his involvement in many work-related organizations. He served as an officer in 16 of them and for his work he received 10 different awards, including the Canadian Horticultural Council's Carter Medal for greatest achievement in horticulture, and an honorary doctorate in science from Acadia University. Moreover, during the time he served as chief of the Horticultural Division it won the American Pomological Society's Wilder Medal seven times for apple-breeding contributions.

Although his work in horticulture was all engrossing, this modest gentleman nevertheless found time to be an active member of the Ottawa Field Naturalists' Club and to serve as an elder of Chalmers United Church. He also served as a commissioner in the Ottawa Improvement Commission (the forerunner of the Federal District Commission, which in turn became the National Capital Commission), from 1920 to 1933.

William Macoun became ill on his annual tour of federal experimental farms in August of 1933. He returned home at the beginning of the month and died there on Sunday, August 13. He was survived by a son, three daughters and a granddaughter, his wife Elizabeth having predeceased him in 1923.

ERIC BROWN

FIRST DIRECTOR OF THE NATIONAL GALLERY OF CANADA

(1877–1939)

———■———

E ric Brown, the first director of Canada's National Gallery, early discovered that it helps to have a clear sense of purpose, determination, nerves of steel and a healthy sense of humour when heading up Canada's leading art gallery.

Fortunately, this tall, slim and elegant figure had all these qualities and more. He was also able to bring shrewdness and enthusiasm to the position of gallery director, which he held from 1910 until his death in Ottawa on April 6, 1939.

Eric Brown appeared to be a most unlikely choice to head up the infant National Gallery as he lacked both a college degree and formal training in the visual arts. Indeed, his preparation for what would be his life's work was, to say the least, unconventional.

The future director was born in Nottingham, England to John Henry Brown, whose country-bred forebears came from the Midlands. Brown Sr., a staunch Conservative, was a city councillor and a founding father of Nottingham University. He was also a lover of the arts and it was in this respect that he exercised a powerful influence on his youngest son Eric.

Eric was only four years old when his mother died, leaving his father with the responsibility of raising nine children. To his rescue came Nurse, who mothered young Eric and helped to shape his manners and morals.

As a result of an unspecified accident on the football field, young Eric had to endure a long illness that prevented him from going to college. During his lengthy convalescence, he spent many hours reading and, under his father's guidance, he eagerly devoured the classics. This helped to develop his love of reading and gift for writing.

Brown's love of literature and his facility for writing would stand him in good stead. So would his penchant for asking pertinent questions and for greedily absorbing information from every available source.

When it came to acquiring knowledge of the visual arts and painting techniques, Eric Brown had to look no further for help than his elder brother Arnesby (later Sir Arnesby), a well-known landscape painter, and Arnesby's wife, Mia, who produced imaginative portraits of children. Both brother and sister-in-law, but especially Arnesby, proved to be a rich source of information and inspiration. According to Eric's wife, Maud, Arnesby's "great honesty and strong convictions made him an excellent teacher for his younger brother."

The knowledge acquired on visits to his brother and sister-in-law in London and during summer sojourns in the St. Ives, Cornwall artists' colony did not pay immediate dividends. After recovering from his illness, Eric Brown found employment not in the visual arts but in agriculture, opting for a job on the tiny Caribbean island of Nevis where he joined a cousin who was growing cotton. When his cousin married, Brown traded in the delightfully casual life on Nevis for farming in Lincolnshire. It was there that he met and became engaged to his future wife, a Cambridge University-educated school teacher.

Shortly after his engagement, Eric Brown went to stay with his brother, Arnesby, at St. Ives, where he met F.R. Heaton, who headed Scott and Son, the Montreal art dealer. Heaton invited Brown to visit him if he ever came to Canada, and shortly thereafter Eric acted on the invitation. No sooner did he and his wife arrive in this country, in 1909, than he found employment in the field to which he would dedicate the remainder of his life, the promotion of Canadian art.

Initially Brown took care of a loan exhibition of British paintings in Montreal. He then went to work for the Art Gallery of Toronto. His stint there was short-lived. Thanks to fortuitous meetings in both cities with Edmund Walker (later Sir Edmund), head of the newly appointed Advisory Arts Council in Ottawa, he was asked to come to the national capital to bring some order into the affairs of the infant National Gallery.

Brown immediately accepted Walker's offer and, in 1910, he was made secretary of the Advisory Arts Council and director of the gallery, an appointment that would not be confirmed until 1913 when the gallery was formally established by an act of Parliament.

When the newly appointed director arrived in Ottawa, the National Gallery was about to move its paintings into the empty east wing of the newly constructed Victoria Museum (now the Museum of Nature). His salary was a mere $100 a month. As a lowly member of the Department of Public Works, serving under its chief architect, he could not order anything—not even a screw driver—without permission.

However, Eric Brown had the good fortune to work closely with Sir Edmund Walker, chairman of the gallery's board of trustees from 1909 to 1924, and a man of vision and kindness. As both men were interested in Canadian art, Brown had the Toronto financier's unfailing support when it came to championing the cause of Canadian art, especially that produced by the Group of Seven, officially formed in 1920.

Eric Brown truly welcomed that support when he both defended and actively promoted the output of this influential group of artists who drew inspiration from the landscapes of Northern Ontario and who, in the 1920's, attracted a lot of controversy because of their break with tradition and their new way of looking at and painting Canada.

When speaking, writing and lecturing about the new movement, recommending the purchase of its works, and displaying its paintings in the National Gallery, Brown brooked opposition from conventionally-minded members of the general public, parliamentarians, the press and various institutions. It was disturbing enough, huffed such critics, that such "immature and raw attempts" at painting should be even seen, but that the National Gallery should exhibit them was beyond belief!

From Halifax to Victoria, the battle raged as letters for and against the movement poured into newspapers, and well-known parliamentarians such as James Woodsworth stood up in the House of Commons to denounce "frightful daubs" in the National Gallery.

Eric Brown's greatest battle, however, was with a determined and conservative Royal Canadian Academy. It had agitated for the establishment of the National Gallery and when the gallery opened the academy assumed control of art purchases and exhibition selections. It performed this role until Eric Brown and his staff began to act independently on such matters, at which point the academy's ire was aroused for it feared losing its grip on these essential functions.

The academy became even more incensed when the gallery director favoured works by the Group of Seven for inclusion in London's British Empire Exhibitions of 1924 and 1925, commonly known as the Wembley

Exhibitions after their north-east London location. In its fight to regain its hegemony, the academy solicited MPs, wrote letters, and staged meetings.

In the year that the Group of Seven was disbanded, 1933, the academy launched what art historian David Silcox has referred to as a bitter "dogfight" over the National Gallery's support of the Group, even calling for Eric Brown's dismissal. As luck would have it, Brown was not dislodged from his position; he was still serving as director when he passed away in April of 1939, having gallantly piloted the gallery safely through resistance to change and artistic orthodoxy to recognition and respect.

MARIUS BARBEAU
ANTHROPOLOGIST, ETHNOLOGIST, FOLKLORIST

(1883–1969)

W hen he died in 1969, just six days before his eighty-sixth birthday, Marius Barbeau was mourned far beyond his native Canada. Not only had he established a reputation as this country's leading anthropologist and folklorist, but he had also played a major role in taking Canadian folklore out of the shadows and in making it better known in Canada and abroad.

Completely bilingual, Barbeau published more than 50 books, twice as many pamphlets and monographs, and some 700 articles in over 100 different periodicals that ran the gamut from scientific journals to daily newspapers and popular magazines. Not content with being an ivory-tower scholar, he worked tirelessly to preserve and promote Canadian folklore in as many ways as he could by teaching, giving lectures, encouraging others to use his material and speaking about his passion on radio and TV.

Born on March 5, 1883, in Ste-Marie-de-Beauce, about 28 miles southeast of Québec City, Marius Barbeau was the first child of Charles Barbeau and Marie-Virginie Morency, both members of well-to-do families whose European ancestors had settled in New France before Ste-Marie was founded in the 1730s.

Barbeau's father, Charles, the son of a land speculator, breeder of race horses and innkeeper, farmed the family's 66-acre family farm, bred champion horses, took part in an abortive gold-hunting expedition in the United States, and dabbled in assorted business ventures in the Beauce. Marie-Virginie, Marius Barbeau's mother, was an educated, refined woman, who had taught music in the St-Joseph-de-Beauce Grey Nuns' convent before deciding not to take her vows to become a nun.

As a child, Marius Barbeau studied music with his mother. His father, who was well versed in French-Canadian folklore—folksongs and folktales— would play the fiddle while Marius performed reels and jigs. His mother, according to her son, "would sit at the piano and sing, and make me sing with her."

When he was 11, Marius and his parents had to decide what he would do with his life. Should he become a farmer and horse breeder like his authoritarian father, whom he feared, or should he become educated like his affectionate, book-loving mother? Marius had no hesitation in announcing, "I go to school."

The youngster received his first taste of formal education at the Collège Commercial de Ste-Marie, Beauce, whose stated aim was to provide a Christian and commercial education that prepared young people for careers in commerce, industry and public administration. The education Barbeau received at this institution was not as memorable, however, as the chance encounter he had there with an Indian priest who travelled from school to school and from parish to parish, providing entertainment that featured Indian songs and dances.

The priest was Abbé Prosper Vincent. When delivering his renditions of old Huron songs to a college audience, he made a deep and lasting impression on young Marius: so much so that the sensitive youngster immediately sensed the opening of a new door.

After completing three years at commercial college, Barbeau took up classical studies at Collège Sainte-Anne-de-la-Pocatière with the intention of becoming a priest. He abandoned this idea in 1903, electing instead to take up law at Laval University, from which he graduated in 1907 at age 23 with a law degree.

Much to his surprise, Barbeau won a Rhodes Scholarship to attend Oxford University. The first French-Canadian scholar so honoured, he spent three years at this venerable institution, switching soon after his arrival from the study of law to the study of anthropology. According to his biographer, Lawrence Nowry, Barbeau would become the earliest Canadian Rhodes Scholar to achieve international recognition in his chosen field.

After he completed his studies at Oxford and summer courses in Paris at the Sorbonne, Barbeau was approached by the renowned Canadian physician and educator, Sir William Osler, then Regius Professor of Medicine at Oxford. Shoving a letter in front of the young man, Osler advised him to return to Canada. "Anthropology is not studied, and there is no one at the Geological Survey. That should be your place there. Make it your own," advised Osler.

Heeding Osler's advice, Barbeau travelled to Ottawa where he was hired in 1911 as anthropologist and ethnologist to the Museum Branch of the

Geological Survey of Canada (in 1927, it became the National Museum, now the Museum of Civilization). He would be employed continuously by the Museum until his retirement in 1949, at which time he became an active consultant, serving the Museum for another 15 years.

Marius Barbeau's first loyalty was to his Québec homeland as the anthropologist and folklorist was convinced that rural Québec had preserved folk traditions dating from medieval times. However, his fascination with Québec's rich store of folklore did not preclude his undertaking many long and arduous field trips in the rest of Canada, and in the United States, conducting research on Indian tribes, notably the Tsimshian in British Columbia.

The first of many field trips was made in the spring of 1911. Equipped with a Standard Edison phonograph and fragile wax cylinders, Barbeau set out to interview Prosper Vincent, then in a home for aged priests in Lorette, Québec. This visit led to the recording of some 60 to 70 Indian songs.

In pursuit of more Huron folklore, Barbeau interviewed Hurons along the Detroit River near Amherstburg and in Oklahoma. One of his more fortunate breaks occurred in 1912 when a 10 to 15-member delegation of Indian chiefs from western Alberta, the Rocky Mountains and the Salish area of the Fraser and Thompson Rivers arrived in Ottawa to discuss land issues with the federal government. Seizing the moment, Marius Barbeau recorded 60 to 70 of their songs.

In 1914, Barbeau attended a meeting of the Anthropological Association in Washington, D.C. It was there that he met Dr. Franz Boas. The celebrated American anthropologist persuaded the young man to return immediately to Lorette, but this time to collect fast-disappearing French-Canadian songs, legends and stories. Barbeau wasted no time in heeding this advice, even expanding his quest to include Charlevoix, Kamouraska and Beauce Counties.

When contemplating all the work he had done among French Canadians and Indian tribes from east to west across Canada, Barbeau once remarked, "I would need two lives to process all my research."

During his lifetime, Marius Barbeau received countless awards for the invaluable role he played in making Canadian folklore better known, and in opening it up to scientific scrutiny. These honours included the presidency of the American Folklore Society (1918), membership in the Royal Canadian Society and appointment to the Order of Canada (1967).

Marius Barbeau died in an Ottawa hospital on February 27, 1969. He was survived by his wife, Marie (née Larocque) and two daughters, Hélène and Dalila.

SELECTED BIBLIOGRAPHY

MANUSCRIPT SOURCES

Library and Archives Canada

George Foster papers MG27-11D7
Freiman Family papers MG30-A82
Trudi Le Caine papers MUS 215
Edward Louis Montizambert and Family papers MG29-C101
Hamnett Pinhey Hill papers MG24-19
Arthur Percy Sherwood papers MG29-C103

Unpublished Works

Cameron, Professor Duncan. Address. Irene Spry.
Spry, Lib. Eulogy. Irene Spry.
Tolgesy, Victor. Journal.

BOOKS

—- *Appreciations*: Hon. Thomas Ahearn, P.C. Privately Printed.

Aberdeen and Temair, Ishbel Gordon, Marchioness of. *The Canadian Journal of Lady Aberdeen*, 1893-1898, edited with an introduction by John T. Saywell. Toronto: Champlain Society, 1960.

Anstey, J.H. *One Hundred Harvests: Research Branch, Agriculture Canada*, 1886-1896. Ottawa: The Branch, 1986.

Banks, Margaret A. *Sir John George Bourinot, Victorian Canadian: His Life, Times and Legacy.* Montreal: McGill-Queen's University Press, 2001.

Brault, Lucien. *Ottawa Old & New.* Ottawa: Ottawa Historical Information Institute, 1946.

Brown, Maud. *Breaking Barriers: Eric Brown and the National Gallery. Ottawa*: The Society for Art Publications, 1964.

The Canadian Encyclopedia, 2nd. edition. Edmonton: Hurtig Publishers, 1988.

Eggleston, Wilfrid. *The Queen's Choice: A Story of Canada's Capital.* Ottawa: The Queen's Printer, 1961.

Forsey, Eugene. *A Life on the Fringe: The Memoirs of Eugene Forsey.* Toronto: Oxford University Press, 1990.

Freiman, Lawrence. *Don't Fall Off the Rocking Horse.* Toronto: McClelland and Stewart, 1978.

Gard, Anson A. *Pioneers of the Upper Ottawa and the Humours of the Valley*, 1906 ed. Reprinted 1999 by Global Heritage Press.

Haig, Robert. *Ottawa: City of the Big Ears.* Ottawa: Haig and Haig, 1970.

Knowles, Valerie. *First Person: A Biography of Cairine Wilson, Canada's First Woman Senator.* Toronto: Dundurn Press, 1988.

Macbeth, Madge. *Over My Shoulder.* Toronto: Ryerson Press, 1954.

Morrison, Cecil. *The Life & Times of G. Cecil Morrison: The Happy Baker of Ottawa. An Autobiography: the Reminiscences of G. Cecil Morrison, 1890-1979, as told to his daughter and son-in-law, Grete and Reg Hale.* Edited by Jenny Wilson. Carp, Ont., 1990.

P.T. Rooke and R.L. Schnell. *No Bleeding Heart: Charlotte Whitton: A Feminist On the Right.* Vancouver: University of British Columbia Press, 1987.

Rose, George, editor. *A Cyclopedia of Canadian Biography: Being Chiefly Men of the Time: A Collection of Persons Distinguished in Professional and Political Life: Leaders in the Commerce and Industry of Canada and Successful Pioneers.* Toronto: Rose Publishing Company, 1886-88.

Ross, Alexander H. D. *Ottawa Past and Present.* Ottawa: Thorburn and Abbott, 1927.

Sanger, Clyde. *Lotta and the Unitarian Service Committee Story.* Toronto: Stoddart, 1986.

Silcox, David P. *The Group of Seven and Tom Thomson*. Toronto: Firefly Books, 2003.

Smith, Helen. *Ottawa's Farm: A History of the Central Experimental Farm*. Burnstown, Ont.: General Store Publishing House, 1996.

Taylor, John. *Ottawa: An Illustrated History*. Toronto: James Lorimer & Company, Publishers, and Canadian Museum of Civilization, 1986.

Tolgesy, Victor. *Acrobatics: A Tale of Fantasy and Reality in Words and Sculpture*. Edited by Naomi Jackson Groves. Ottawa: Edahl Productions, c 1985.

Walker, Harry and Olive. *Carleton Saga*. Ottawa: Published by the authority of Carleton County, 1971.

Williams, David Ricardo. *Duff: A Life in the Law*. Vancouver: University of British Columbia Press in association with the Osgoode Society, 1984.

Woods Jr., Shirley E. *Ottawa The Capital of Canada*. Toronto: Doubleday Canada Limited, 1980.

Young, Gayle. *The Sackbut Blues: Hugh Le Caine Pioneer in Electronic Music*. Ottawa: National Museum of Science and Technology, c 1989.

ARTICLES

Barbeau, Marius. "The Folklorist," www.civilization.ca/academ/barbeau/bafleng.html

Barbeau, Marius. "The Student," www.civilization.ca/academ/barbeau/basteng.html

Benidickson, Jamie. Article on John R. Booth, *Dictionary of Canadian Biography* online.

Brown, R. Blake. "The Supreme Court of Canada and Judicial Legitimacy in the Rise and Fall of Chief Justice Lyman Poor Duff." *McGill Law Journal*, March 2003.

Bush, Edward F. "Thomas Coltrin Keefer," *Ontario History*, vol. 66, no. 4, 1974.

Clarke, Brian P. Article on Richard William Scott, *Dictionary of Canadian Biography* online.

Cook, Sharon Anne. Article on Lady Foster, *Dictionary of Canadian Biography* online.

Gillis, Robert Peter. Article on Henry F. Bronson. *Dictionary of Canadian Biography* online.

Gouglas, Sean. Article on Collingwood Schreiber, *Dictionary of Canadian Biography* online.

Kelly, Peggy. "Cultural Nationalism and Maternal Feminism: Madge Macbeth as Writer, Broadcaster and Literary Figure." *Framing Our Past in Canadian Women's History in the Twentieth Century*. Edited by Sharon Anne Cook, Lorna R. McLean and Kate O'Rourke. Montreal: McGill-Queen's University Press, c 2001.

Laurentian Leadership Centre. "John R. Booth - Businessman." www.twu.ca/laurentian/History/BBusiness.asp

Nelles, H.V. Article on Thomas C. Keefer. *Dictionary of Canadian Biography* online.

Simpson, Janice C. "Healing the Wound: Cultural Compromise in D.C. Scott's 'A Scene at Lake Manitou.'" www.arts.uwo.ca/canpoetry/cpjrn/vol18/simpson.htm

Seccareccia, Mario. "Irene Spry (1907-1998) Obituary." www.yorku.ca/cwen/spry.htm

NEWSPAPERS

The *Gazette* (Montreal)

The Globe (Toronto)

The *Ottawa Citizen*

The *Ottawa Evening Journal*

The Ottawa Journal

The *Ottawa Evening Journal*

PHOTOGRAPHY CREDITS

COA = City of Ottawa Archives
NAC = National Archives of Canada (now known as Library and Archives Canada)
USC = Unitarian Service Committee

Thomas Ahearn	COA
Marius Barbeau	NAC C34447
Henry F. Bronson	COA
John G. Bourinot	NAC PA 271119
Eric Brown	NAC PA 120859
Moss Kent Dickinson	COA
Lyman Duff	NAC PA 124813
Harold Fisher	COA
Sandford Fleming	NAC PA 42840
Eugene Forsey	NAC PA 120736
Lady Foster	NAC PA 27773
Lillian Freiman	NAC PA 105077
Hamnett Hill	COA
Lotta Hitschmanova	USC Canada
Thomas Keefer	COA
Hamnett Kirkes Pinhey	COA
Trudi Le Caine	Cynthia Durance
Madge Macbeth	COA
William Macoun	NAC PA 136873
Frederick Montizambert	NAC C 56126
G. Cecil Morrison	Photographer not indentified
Collingwood Schreiber	NAC PA 277791
Arthur Percy Sherwood	NAC C 449004
Irene Spry	Richard Spry
Duncan Campbell Scott	NAC C 39958
Richard Scott	COA
Victor Tolgesy	Grethe Tolgesy
Cairine Wilson	Karsh, Ottawa
Alexander S. Woodburn	COA
William Wylie	NAC PA 213866

INDEX